Cranks

FASTFOOD

Cranks
FASTFOOD

Nadine Abensur

CASSELL&CO

For Barry
And for Digby and Noah

First published in the United Kingdom
in 2000 by Cassell & Co

Distributed in the United States of America by
Sterling Publishing Co, Inc
387 Park Avenue South, New York, NY 10016-8810

A CIP catalogue record for this book is available
from the British Library

ISBN 0 304 35606 9

Design Director: David Rowley
Design: Clive Hayball/Miranda Harvey
Photography: Philip Webb
Food stylists: Bridget Sargeson, Nadine Abensur

Colour separation by Tenon & Polert Colour Scanning Ltd

Printed and bound in France

Cassell & Co
Wellington House
125 Strand
London WC2R 0BB

contents

introduction

These are recipes I cook at home – they are not based on some **fantasy** lifestyle. They are my lifestyle. I cook like this because, until recently, like many women, I worked full time and had a young child. I was never home before 7pm, often later. It has always been up to me to prepare the food. My husband is an **alien** in the **kitchen**, with practically no interest in food except what is put in front of him – but he is hugely appreciative of that, I must say.

This is far less of a hardship to me than I might be making it sound. In fact, I thoroughly enjoy cooking. That half hour or so in the kitchen makes me feel that I am home. It brings everything together. It **unites** and **harmonizes**.

When the idea of a Cranks fast food book originally came up, everyone was wildly enthusiastic. 'Fast' has, after all, been the **buzz** word of the last decade. But I tried to wriggle out of it. 'I might live like this but I don't believe in it,' I cried. 'I only make my casserole with canned chickpeas because I have to, not because I think that's how it should be done.' 'Does it taste good?' my editor asked. 'Well, yes, actually, it **tastes fab**.' 'What's the problem then?' she replied. Still, there remained a little niggling doubt.

Once we settled the 30 minutes optimum time rule, I set to testing. There ensued some frantic scenes in the kitchen with my assistant, Annabel, and I meticulously timing everything.

Does 'a couple' mean two minutes or three? Am I going to be had up under the Trades Descriptions Act? Do I have to teach people how to hold a knife, to be able to chop as fast as a pro? This is why I had been uneasy. Was I going to be held responsible for every second away from prime time television?

So, rather than tear our hair out, we relaxed. We laughed. We enjoyed ourselves. 'This is how cooking should be,' we said. **Pleasure**. **Fun**. And at the end of the day, we found that we had made a multitude of recipes – not the usual five or six you expect to test in one day, but 11, 12, or 13. Yes, these recipes really were **quick**. And **delicious**. Once in a while, we got bogged down in something that felt a little too laboured, too much like hard work. We left it out.

I asked Annabel, 'When would you eat this? Lunch? Evening? Would you eat it alone or would you feel **comfortable** making it for a crowd?' I tried to take all this into account. Can the recipes be easily replicated for larger numbers, and quickly? In most cases, yes, though they might take slightly longer. Many **fast food** books seem aimed at eating alone or, at most, with one other. In this book, I kept families in mind too.

By far the majority of these recipes are **naturally**, intrinsically quick to prepare. But for others I haven't been shy to use a little help – relatively old-fashioned help, such as a pressure cooker; I still refuse to own a microwave. I want to stand over a **hot stove**. Maybe not for hours on end, but I want to get my hands dirty, I want to stick my nose in a big bunch of fresh coriander and **inhale**. I want to see things **sizzle**, char, crisp and braise. I want the smells. Most of the recipes in this book will yield these aplenty.

There are recipes that you might not associate with fast food at all. Gratins, for instance, might traditionally take hours to prepare, layer up and **bake** slowly. Some might say that they have no place in this book, that they need too much tinkering with and are therefore no longer 'authentic'. I am just not prepared to give them up. A long time ago I realized I could speed up the cooking process and I promise they are no less delicious. Perhaps only a little less formal.

I use shop-bought, chilled puff pastry with no sense of guilt, and much sense of **satisfaction** when a fabulous tart can land on the table a mere 30 minutes later. I have no qualms about using frozen vegetables: petits pois, broad beans, spinach, sweetcorn and artichoke bottoms.

I buy good-quality pestos when I can, but these can be pretty pricey and fast food should not necessarily mean expensive food, and so I have suggested a series of **storecupboard** items to have to hand, or prepare on a lazy Sunday afternoon. Some will keep for weeks at a time.

You will see that at least a third of the recipes in this book show **inspiration** from Morocco, the Middle East and the eastern Mediterranean. It would have been easy to include more of these, but I wanted to cover a broader spectrum. We have become so **multi-cultural** in our eating habits that I wanted to reflect this and to include a wide range of **irresistible** recipes – some quite intense, others more gentle.

storecupboard

Here is a by no means exhaustive list of the condiments and spices that I am rarely without in the kitchen, all of which help me to get delicious food on to the table in next to no time.

almonds Whole with their skins on: it takes only a minute to blanch them and the skins come off easily – a perfect in-front-of-the-television activity. In fact, only one recipe in this book actually asks you to do this; for the rest, toasted and slivered is perfect.

artichokes Bottled, frozen or even canned.

balsamic vinegar The best is divine, aged for up to 30 years and very expensive. The cheapest is not balsamic vinegar at all, in that it has not been aged, but the flavour simply approximated with caramel (I still find it better than nothing – just about).

bouillon powder Marigold is the brand I use for quick stocks and soups.

brandy I keep it in the freezer (though anywhere would do) with my bottle of Cointreau and my bottle of vodka. I add a glug to cream and other sauces, and to many desserts.

chickpeas and cannellini beans in cans. Perfect for using in casseroles and salads. But also drained and blended or mashed to make houmous – smooth or rough – with olive oil, added slowly, until it won't take any more, usually four tablespoons, plus two tablespoons of the liquid from the can, a clove of crushed garlic, a pinch of ground cumin and a dash of Tabasco. Lemon juice can go in it or be served with it. Stuff into warm pitta bread or scoop into Little Gem lettuce leaves; serve on the side with tabouleh; or thin with a little water and pour over salads as a dressing in its own right.

chillies Red, usually bird's eye, as others seem to have had the heat bred out of them. Green, only if I am planning a Thai green curry.

coriander Large bunches from Middle Eastern food shops. Stand the bunch of coriander in a jar or glass of water and keep it in the fridge to substantially increase its shelf life and to keep the leaves plump and fresh.

couscous For use in recipes, but also just to soak and pour olive oil over, with fresh coriander, a squeeze of harissa, a finely chopped tomato and not much else.

cumin I could not cook without cumin, ground and in seed form. It adds a pungent, earthy, warming note to all it comes near. It turns a Mediterranean kitchen into a Moorish, deeply exotic one. It even makes carrots sexy.

eggs Large, organic, free range – the way they all should be, and perhaps the way they all could be if only we chose to eat 'real' food again. Dream on.

ful medames Cooked and canned dried broad beans, usually quite salty. They need only a lick of olive oil, a squeeze of lemon juice and a lump of crushed garlic to provide a filling lunch. Just remember to chew well.

garlic I buy it every time I go shopping – I'm so afraid of running out! And if I know I've got a busy cooking schedule I peel a whole lot and cover it with plenty of olive oil. It lasts a few days in the fridge and the oil is incredibly useful.

harissa Several of the recipes in this book call for a side dish of harissa, the fiery Tunisian chilli paste. You can buy a very good one in tubes or small cans – the packaging looks exactly the same now as it has done for decades. It is made with hot, dried red chillies, fresh garlic, caraway or fennel seeds, and dried coriander seeds, all pounded together to a paste and sometimes finished off with fresh mint and coriander. I also make it with fresh chillies and an inauthentic, but I think delicious, sprinkling of cumin. It is available in most Middle Eastern food shops and increasingly in supermarkets. And please try it with less obvious suggestions too – anything in the egg chapter for instance.

lemons and limes The thin-skinned ones are better for juicing, the thicker better for preserving (page 17). Unwaxed, organic lemons are lovely, but watch like a hawk – they only last a couple of days out of the fridge, and if one begins to go mouldy the others next to it in a bowl will follow suit faster than you can squeeze a lemon. Refrigerate and they should last a week or two.

miso Fermented soya bean paste, sold vacuum-packed in health food shops, lasts for months in the fridge.

mustard Grain and Dijon, though I still love bright yellow, fiery, eye-stinging English mustard. I use it regularly for my mother's vinaigrette (page 16)

oil, groundnut For shallow and, especially, deep frying. Almost tasteless in the widely available varieties. But you can make it more interesting by adding a few toasted peanuts when cooking with it.

oils, olive A light, fruity one from Liguria, and a deep green, extra virgin one from Tuscany, especially for eating raw. It is best to buy top quality oils, but I have lost count of the times I've just bought average ones. I don't think my cooking suffers for it. Many cooks would kill me but a) I can't always justify the expense and b) to paraphrase a common saying, a bad cook always blames his ingredients. A good, sensitive cook can make anything taste fantastic!

olives Large, juicy, kalamata olives are wonderful. I also love French Provençal, marinated in herbs. Lemon-stuffed olives from Middle Eastern shops are refreshing and light. Moroccan olives are salty, the black ones are quite dry – an acquired taste (I've acquired it). New to me and absolutely delicious are the Luc Royale green olives. They are long and thin and, for an olive, mild and delicate. I also keep jars of olive purées, green and black. Sometimes I stuff 10 or 15 pitted olives into a piece of warmed baguette, nothing else added. Delicious!

onions and shallots How many recipes start with the familiar refrain, 'Heat some oil in a pan and fry some chopped onions until translucent/golden brown'? Occasionally I've had to cook for people who didn't eat onions. It was like cooking with no nose.

paprika Bought in large bags from Middle Eastern or Indian shops, it should be bright red. I prefer the sweet varieties but some like the very pungent; there is also a smoked paprika that, if you are not careful, is rather overwhelming. Paprika blends fantastically with cumin for Moorish recipes. As with all spices, keep well sealed in a dark, cool place.

parmesan Is there an ode? There should be. Parmigiano Reggiano has the fullest flavour. Buy a block of it and grate as you need it. I brought back an enormous block of it from Italy, wrapped in wax paper, and didn't regret it for a minute. Do not waste your money on the tubs of powdered debris.

pasta Spaghetti, linguine (which can often be found in small local shops and, of course, Italian delis), pappardelle, orecchiette (little ears) or cavatelli (small rolled-up pieces), found as above.

pernod Lives under the stairs and occasionally comes out to liven up fennel.

pesto I usually make this myself, not always conventionally (page 15).

polenta Made from corn (and about the only use Italians make of this crop). Fast cooking – and my health-conscientious streak be damned, add lots and lots of butter, Parmesan and olive oil and pour into a light bouillon.

rice Basmati, basmati and basmati for anything east of anywhere. For risotti, arborio is the most versatile, carnaroli is the creamiest, vialone nano is the fastest cooking. Italian organic short-grain brown rice for times of necessary abstention and clean out, for welcome days of simplicity and also surprisingly good for paella. Quick-cook brown rice, believe it or not, again for paella, and proper short-grain paella rice when it can be found.

saffron The Spanish or Sardinian filaments or stamens are the best. They come from the crocus flower – it takes half a million flowers to produce 1 kg/2 lb 4 oz of saffron. Keep them cool and wrapped up. I don't see the point of the powdered stuff. It's cheaper but you have to use more.

sea salt Big flakes to crush between your fingers for cooking and salads. Pouring salt for baking.

sun-dried tomatoes Because they get me out of trouble every time. Blend until smooth or just use a good bright red purée – just as indispensable – and add to double cream for one of the simplest and most delicious pasta sauces. Also slow-roasted or sun-blushed tomatoes, not as dry, nor as salty and very easy to make for yourself (page 16).

tamari This is simply a very pure soya sauce with – unlike more widely available varieties – no wheat added. It appears in almost every recipe in this book: used judiciously, it adds the depth and roundness of flavour that I seek.

tamarind paste A delicious, semi-sharp, sweetish pulp from a tropical pod. The seeds are turned into a thick dried paste which may need to be reconstituted with water, though it is also available reconstituted and ready for use. You don't get as much bang for your buck that way but for the sake of ease it is this I refer to in this book.

truffle oil I don't claim to keep a bottle of the really expensive oil, though if someone wants to buy me one for Christmas… Otherwise, I use the much lighter form available in delis and supermarkets. It does mean that I use it as I would olive oil, whereas with the real thing only a few drops suffice. It's up to you.

white wine vinegar I don't use it often except in dressings, but it's always there.

wine This has always been difficult because my husband, Digby, doesn't drink at all and as for me, one drop and I'm away. I love to cook with it, so I am truly grateful to Nigella Lawson, who suggests freezing it in glassfuls. I have always kept my other rarely used tipples in the freezer but had never thought to do this with wine.

storecupboard secrets

Here are some delicious sauces and dressings that can be served in next to no time on a typically exhausting weekday. Take a lazy Sunday afternoon and enjoy preparing them in advance.

basil pesto

2 plump garlic cloves, very finely
  chopped or crushed
60 g/2 oz pine nuts
60 g/2 oz very fresh basil, including stems
60 g/2 oz Parmesan, freshly grated
150 ml/5 fl oz light olive oil
sea salt

Using a pestle and mortar, pound the garlic and pine nuts together, then add the basil leaves, a few at a time, grinding them to a pulp against the side of the bowl. Stir in the grated cheese, then slowly add the olive oil, beating as you do so. Season with a little sea salt.

watercress pesto

90 g/3 oz watercress, tough stalks
  removed, and chopped
4 tablespoons light olive oil
1 teaspoon balsamic vinegar
4–6 garlic cloves, chopped
1 shallot, very finely chopped
1 tablespoon ground almonds (optional)
sea salt

I prefer to mix this by hand as I don't want it to become too much of a purée. Mix all the ingredients and serve with pasta, on grilled vegetables or on toast.

coriander pesto

1 large bunch of coriander
  (about 180 g/6 oz), leaves only
2 tablespoons whole almonds
6 garlic cloves, finely chopped or crushed
4 tablespoons light olive oil
juice of 1 lime
½ teaspoon Tabasco sauce
1 cm/½ inch piece of red chilli, chopped
  very small
sea salt

Chop the coriander with a very sharp knife. Pound the almonds in a pestle and mortar or chop in a food processor. Mix these two ingredients with the garlic and then add the remaining ingredients and a pinch of salt.

quick tomato pesto

12 slow-roasted tomato quarters
  (see next page)
30 g/1 oz Parmesan, freshly grated
1 tablespoon olive oil
2 garlic cloves, crushed
4–5 basil leaves
sea salt and freshly ground black pepper

Blend the tomatoes, Parmesan, oil and garlic. Tear in the basil and add salt and pepper. Use instead of tomato sauce, as a garnish to soups or on toast topped with a poached egg. This makes about 150 g/5 oz, or 2 generous servings

my mother's vinaigrette

This makes a thick, yellow, mustardy dressing quite unlike most people's perceptions of vinaigrette. It transforms plain iceberg lettuce and is great with artichokes or asparagus. I make a batch every few weeks and keep it in a large jar. If you want to do the same, simply triple or quadruple the quantities given below.

1 dessertspoon English mustard
4 tablespoons olive or sunflower oil
1 garlic clove, crushed
1 teaspoon white wine vinegar
small pinch of salt and freshly ground
    black pepper

Put the mustard in a bowl and trickle in the oil very slowly, beating continuously with a fork until thoroughly mixed in. Add the garlic and vinegar and beat vigorously. Season lightly with salt and pepper. For a quick method, place all the ingredients in a jar with a tight lid and shake very well.

vinaigrette with olive oil, balsamic vinegar and grain mustard

1 teaspoon balsamic vinegar
1 dessertspoon wholegrain mustard
4 tablespoons olive oil
small pinch of salt and freshly ground
    black pepper
sprig of tarragon (optional)
1 garlic clove, crushed (optional)

Add the vinegar to the mustard in a jar or bottle, then pour in the oil, season with salt and pepper and shake. Add a sprig of tarragon if you like, and the garlic.

slow-roasted tomato quarters

I recommend vine tomatoes because quite often those left on the vine look redder and juicier than their cellophane-wrapped cousins, but it might just be my imagination and I may be being duped by the romantic name. It is true that I've often bought big bunches of them from Middle Eastern food shops, where they are not only cheaper, but really do look and taste better.

850 g/1 lb 14 oz vine tomatoes, cut
    into quarters
3 tablespoons olive oil
1 teaspoon sea salt flakes
handful of fresh basil, roughly chopped
2 garlic cloves, thinly sliced
pinch of soft brown sugar
1 teaspoon balsamic vinegar

Preheat the oven to 190°C/375°F/gas 5. Generously coat the tomato quarters with the other ingredients and roast for an hour, then switch off and leave in the oven to cool. They will keep in an airtight container for several weeks. Use them in sauces and salads, or with pasta.

can be served in next

chermoula

This magnificent sauce (traditionally served with fish but excellent with vegetables) will hugely expand your culinary repertoire. It is one of the richest, most complex, yet at the same time most versatile of sauces. It is composed of all the ingredients used in the Moorish and Middle Eastern recipes in this book, but by existing as a sauce in its own right it gives you endless options.

1 large bunch of coriander, tough stalks removed, very finely chopped
1 large bunch of parsley, tough stalks removed, very finely chopped
6 large garlic cloves, very finely chopped or crushed
1–2 tablespoons ground cumin
1 tablespoon sweet paprika
good pinch of cayenne or ½–1 teaspoon harissa
juice of 2 lemons
300 ml/10 fl oz extra virgin olive oil

Mix all the ingredients together. This makes a large amount but it keeps well in a sealed container (be careful – it can completely take over your fridge if not covered properly).

preserved lemons

Here is an easy, manageable recipe that will last you up to several weeks. Serve the lemons with cold drinks, chopped into green olives, or simply on the side with any of the Moroccan and Moorish inspired recipes in this book. Blended with olive oil and a little crushed garlic, they also make a delicious and unusual dressing.

3 whole lemons, thick skinned and unwaxed
3 tablespoons sea salt
juice of 3 lemons

Cut the lemons, but not all the way through, into quarters, so they are still attached at the stem end. Fill them with salt and place in a preserving jar – with a rubber seal, if possible. Add any remaining salt on top. Leave for 3 days. By then they will have begun to soften and weep some of their juices. Cover them with the juice of the 3 lemons. Reseal and set aside in a cool dark place for about a month before you use them.

'Delicious sauces and dressings that to no time on a typically exhausting weekday'

1

Amazing antipasti and other snacks

I like the mezze, tapas, antipasti approach – delicious morsel after delicious morsel of this and that. For others, a starter is a measured entry into a meal. And for all of us, one of these light, simple dishes is often all we need.

Goat's cheese with extra virgin olive oil

My friends Anjalika and Azeema eat this for breakfast and so, despite my husband's grimace, do I. He is strictly a porridge man. But then he is a Kiwi and I am a Mediterranean through and through. The goat's cheese is the soft stuff that comes in little pots that look like sandcastles. Medium fat is as high as it needs to be, what with all that olive oil.

For a light lunch or brunch, add a ripe tomato or two, some black olives and a chunk of warmed bread.

SERVES 2–4
150 g/5 oz mild creamy goat's cheese
4 tablespoons (at least) extra virgin olive oil
sea salt and freshly ground black pepper

What can I say? Simply divide the goat's cheese between the plates, flatten with the back of a spoon and drizzle the olive oil over. Break up a few flakes of sea salt over the top, sprinkle on a little cracked black pepper and away you go.

'For a light lunch or brunch, add a ripe tomato or two, some black

Sweet potato chips with coriander pesto

The last time I made these I left them in the fridge thinking I would bring them out again the next day, but by then there were none left as I or my husband picked at them every time we opened the fridge. So hot or cold, today or tomorrow, it doesn't really matter.

SERVES 4
1 kg/2 lb 4 oz sweet potatoes in their skins, scrubbed and sliced into chips
3 tablespoons olive oil
sea salt and freshly ground black pepper
4 tablespoons coriander pesto (page 15)

Preheat the oven to its highest setting.

Spread the potato chips in a roasting tin, pour the oil over them, then sprinkle with sea salt and freshly ground black pepper.

Roast for 25 minutes, until crisp in places, then remove from the oven. Transfer to a dish and carefully mix with the coriander pesto.

olives and a chunk of warmed bread'

Baguette with artichoke, olive tapenade, mozzarella and rocket

The kind of snack the Italians serve mid-afternoon, when restaurants are closed till much later, but better because of the baguette or other rustic loaf rather than the typical Italian panini.

SERVES 4
1 baguette
4 tablespoons green olive paste
8 artichoke hearts, roasted and bottled in olive oil
150 g/5 oz mozzarella, sliced
2 tablespoons olive oil
freshly ground black pepper
4 handfuls of rocket
dash of best balsamic vinegar

Preheat the oven to its highest setting.

Break the baguette in half and then slice each half lengthways. Spread a tablespoon of green olive paste onto each quarter. Cut the artichoke hearts in half through the top and divide equally between the baguette quarters. Toss the mozzarella slices in a tablespoon of olive oil and divide between the pieces of baguette.

Bake in the hot oven until the mozzarella is melted, about 5–7 minutes, and then season with black pepper.

Toss the rocket in the remaining olive oil and the balsamic vinegar; serve the rocket either on the side or piled on top.

Smoked aubergines with lemon and garlic

If you are lucky enough to have a stove – I am assuming a gas stove – with more than one large ring you'll be able to smoke several aubergines at a time. However, even one at a time, at about seven minutes each if you choose long thin aubergines, you won't break the time bank.

Delicious with warm bread or, to make this into the sort of Moorish-inspired first course I am seeing on more and more restaurant menus, serve it with the Broad beans with cumin, paprika and olive oil (opposite) or another bean salad, similarly dressed or just doused with olive oil and lemon. If you have some chermoula (page 17) in the fridge or are planning a Moroccan-inspired meal, adding a spoonful of it to the aubergines would raise the stakes.

SERVES 2
2 long, quite thin aubergines
2–3 tablespoons olive oil, to taste
juice of half a lemon
dash of Tabasco sauce
sea salt
1 large garlic clove, very thinly sliced
a few basil or coriander leaves, shredded

Place a wire rack or oven shelf (an old one you don't care too much about is best as it will buckle in the heat) over a high flame and put an aubergine (or two) on top.

The skin will soon start to char. Regularly turn the aubergine so that it becomes black and charred all over. Prick with a fork to test that the flesh is completely soft inside – it should offer no resistance at all.

Take the aubergine off the heat and then slice lengthways at 1 cm/½ inch intervals, stopping short of going all the way through. Return to the heat and smoke for another minute or so, turning carefully. If you are doing them one at a time, transfer the first aubergine to a plate while you smoke the second one.

Mix together the olive oil, lemon juice, Tabasco and salt and drizzle over the aubergines, making sure the mixture goes between the slices.

Garnish with the finely sliced garlic and shredded basil or coriander and serve with warmed pitta or flat bread.

Broad beans with cumin, paprika and olive oil

A pungent, robust dish – no need to peel the broad beans. Serve as part of a Middle Eastern/Mediterranean meal.

SERVES 2
375 g/13 oz frozen broad beans
3 tablespoons olive oil
1 tablespoon ground cumin
1 tablespoon paprika, good and red, plus a little extra for serving
1 garlic clove, crushed
dash of Tabasco sauce
1 teaspoon tamari
sea salt and freshly ground black pepper
3 tablespoons Greek yoghurt
few small sprigs of coriander, to garnish
1 lemon, cut into wedges

Bring a pan of salted water to the boil. Cook the broad beans for 6–7 minutes.

Meanwhile, heat the oil in a heavy-bottomed saucepan or frying pan over a gentle heat. Fry the cumin and paprika, adding a couple of tablespoons of water to stop them burning and darkening too much, and then add the garlic. Stir constantly, adding more water as soon as the last is absorbed, until the mixture resembles a thick paste.

Drain the broad beans, reserving some of their water, and immediately add them to the spice mixture in the pan. Add the Tabasco and tamari and season to taste.

Cook for about 2 more minutes, adding a little of the reserved broad bean water if the mixture becomes too dry.

Serve in a bowl with the Greek yoghurt, either on top or served on the side, sprinkled with a little paprika, the coriander and lemon wedges.

Roasted tomatoes
with parsley, breadcrumbs and garlic

As an antipasti, this needs little other than bread by the side. For a light lunch, I'll eat this with a bowl of green vegetables, blanched or griddled as appropriate, some basmati rice and a bottle of good olive oil to hand. For a fuller lunch or light garden supper, serve with the Smoked aubergines (page 24). Because one happens while the other takes care of itself, you will be in and out of the kitchen in the same brief time.

SERVES 2–4
8 tomatoes, about 500 g/1 lb 2 oz, cut in half horizontally
4 garlic cloves, crushed
50 g/1½ oz breadcrumbs
3 tablespoons chopped fresh parsley
sea salt and freshly ground black pepper
3 tablespoons Parmesan or Emmental, grated
1 tablespoon olive oil

Preheat the oven to 200°C/400°F/gas 6.

Place the tomato halves in an ovenproof dish, cut side up.

Using your hands, mix together the garlic, breadcrumbs, parsley, salt and pepper. Divide this mixture equally over the tomatoes, sprinkle with the cheese and the olive oil, then place in the oven until lightly browned, about 15 minutes. Serve immediately.

'For a light garden supper, serve with the smoked aubergines'

Grilled courgettes with lemon and yoghurt

Claudia Roden gives a recipe for courgettes and yoghurt with mint in her book (the most wonderful cookery book ever written) *A History of Jewish Food*, but despite being born in Morocco, I am not partial to mint. However, I do love grilled courgettes and eat them often (I've also griddled them – you decide). I have served this as a starter, as an accompaniment to the Saffron potato, spinach and Fontina cheese pie (page 120), and as lunch with Arabic bread and a salad of tomatoes, celery and cucumber cut very small and mixed with a spoonful of capers and coarsely chopped parsley.

SERVES 4
4 large courgettes, about 500 g/1 lb 2 oz, cut lengthways into slices ½ cm/¼ inch thick
3 tablespoons light olive oil
sea salt and freshly ground black pepper
350 ml/12 fl oz Greek yoghurt
juice of half a lemon
1 garlic clove, crushed
fresh mint or basil to garnish (optional)
1 tablespoon pine nuts, lightly toasted, or pistachios, roughly broken

Preheat the grill or a large griddle pan. Brush the courgettes on both sides with olive oil and a little crushed sea salt. Spread out on a baking sheet and grill – or cook them on the hot griddle – until pleasantly browned or charred on both sides.

Meanwhile, mix the yoghurt with the lemon juice and garlic.

Leave the courgettes to cool down a little (or the yoghurt will run), then layer them on a dinner plate or shallow serving dish, four or five slices on each layer, spooning on enough yoghurt to cover each time, until you run out of courgettes and yoghurt. Garnish with the mint or basil and the pine nuts or pistachios. If you can let it stand for even a few minutes, so much the better, if not, tuck in.

Palm hearts Réunionien with saffron, garlic and chilli

A little while ago, at my friends Harriet and Steve's wedding, I sat next to someone who asked whether I knew of the French *département* Réunion, where he and his wife had just spent a memorable week. 'Well, no, I don't think so,' I replied. That night my husband, Digby, and I boarded the train for a weekend in Paris. The next evening we were meandering through the streets of Montparnasse when I saw a sign pointing into the smallest of side streets. Restaurant Réunionien, it said. Well, kismet or I don't know what, but five minutes later we were seated at our table, on an evening so balmy we might have been on that small island itself. For a starter, I had Palm hearts Réunionien. Here it is.

SERVES 2
1 tablespoon olive oil
2 garlic cloves, thinly sliced
400 g/14 oz can palm hearts, drained and cut in half lengthways
1 cm/½ inch red chilli, very finely chopped
good pinch of saffron, dissolved in 120 ml/4 fl oz boiling water
1 small ripe tomato, blanched, peeled, deseeded and chopped (optional)

Heat the oil in a heavy-bottomed saucepan or frying pan and fry the garlic over a gentle heat without letting it colour at all.

Add the palm hearts and chilli. Sauté for a minute, gently shaking the pan.

Add the saffron stock, a little at a time. Cook over a high heat and let the stock evaporate before adding a little more. If the palm hearts are sticking, add extra water a little at a time, stopping when there is just enough golden saffron sauce to coat the bottom of the pan. The palm hearts, meanwhile, will be softening and breaking up a little but that's exactly as I ate them. If you prefer the hearts to retain more of their shape, cook them on a gentler heat and stop a little sooner. At the very end, add the chopped tomato, if using, and serve warm.

Walnut and raisin toasts with two toppings

A Saturday lunch, thrown together twixt picking up dry cleaning and supermarket shopping, knowing we were going out for dinner that night. I had a ready-roasted half butternut squash in the fridge, but even starting from scratch this is very quick.

SERVES 4
1 small butternut squash, rounded end only
1 tablespoon olive oil
1 teaspoon tamari
dash of Tabasco sauce
8 slices of walnut and raisin bread
8 teaspoons pesto, any kind
1 small firm but ripe avocado, sliced
12–16 pieces of slow-roasted tomato quarters (page 16)

Preheat the oven to 200°C/400°F/gas 6. Peel the butternut squash, scoop out and discard the seeds, then slice into thin half moons, approximately ½ cm/¼ inch thick.

Mix the olive oil, tamari and Tabasco together, then brush over the butternut squash slices. Place in an ovenproof dish and roast in the hot oven for about 15–20 minutes or until tender.

When you are ready, toast the bread and spread with the pesto. On four of the toasts arrange three or four butternut squash slices and top with a little more pesto. On the other four toasts, arrange the avocado and top with a few pieces of roasted tomato.

Serve two of each toast per person.

Tabouleh with chickpeas
with cucumber and garlic tzatziki

Adding chickpeas to tabouleh turns a snack or side dish into a one-plate meal and with thick garlic yoghurt, a mini-feast. If authenticity is what you are after, use small young lettuce leaves to scoop it up and eat it with.

SERVES 4
180 g/6 oz medium coarse bulgar (or cracked) wheat
400 g/14 oz can chickpeas, drained
500 g/1 lb 2 oz firm ripe tomatoes, diced small
juice of 1 large lemon, to taste
4 spring onions, thinly sliced
very large bunch of flat-leafed parsley, roughly chopped
bunch of mint or coriander (about 60 g/2 oz), chopped
6 tablespoons extra virgin olive oil
sea salt and freshly ground black pepper
4 Little Gem lettuces, leaves separated, for serving

tzatziki
250 ml/8 fl oz Greek yoghurt
½ cucumber, coarsely grated, salted and left to drain
2 garlic cloves, crushed
1 tablespoon chopped fresh mint or coriander

Put the bulgar wheat in a bowl and add boiling water just to cover (this will be the same volume of water as there is bulgar wheat). Leave for 15–20 minutes.

Add the rest of the ingredients (except for the lettuce leaves). Mix gently and allow to settle for a few minutes.

For the tzatziki, mix together all the ingredients in a serving bowl.

Serve the bowl of tabouleh with the bowl of tzatziki, and the lettuce leaves on a separate plate, for people to scoop up the tabouleh.

Buckwheat with herbs and olive oil
– and an egg thrown in

A great alternative to brown rice, with the same grounding attributes – so perfect as an antidote to rich food – but cooked in a fraction of the time. I like buckwheat and a bowl of green vegetables as much as any grander thing.

SERVES 4
4 tablespoons olive oil
2 spring onions, finely chopped
1 garlic clove, very finely chopped or crushed
350 g/12 oz buckwheat
2 teaspoons tamari
dash of Tabasco sauce
2 large free range eggs
juice of half a lemon
sea salt and freshly ground black pepper
2–3 tablespoons roughly chopped mixed parsley and chives
8 or more dried porcini slices, soaked in a little boiling water with a dash of tamari
1 tablespoon nori seaweed flakes (optional)
1 tablespoon sesame seeds

Heat half the olive oil in a heavy-bottomed saucepan or frying pan and add one of the spring onions and the garlic. Sauté until translucent.

Add the buckwheat and stir. Fry for a few minutes, until it is well coated in the oil and begins to give off its characteristic earthy smell.

Add enough boiling water to cover, then add the tamari and Tabasco, lower the heat, cover and cook for about 10 minutes.

Beat the eggs in a bowl with the lemon juice, salt, pepper and most of the herbs.

The buckwheat should be soft and fully expanded; some of it will be a little mushy but that's okay. If it hasn't reached this stage, add more water and continue cooking until it is all absorbed.

Add the porcini, then quickly stir in the egg mixture and continue stirring until the egg scrambles. Remove from the heat, stir in the rest of the olive oil and immediately serve into four bowls; garnish with the nori flakes if using, sesame seeds and the remaining spring onion and herbs.

Soups, laksas and one-bowl meals

Ditch the cans. Forget the cartons. Throw away the packet and get with the blender. You may have convinced yourself that shop-bought is just as good but it ain't. And if you forget how to make soup you may as well forget how to tie your own shoelaces.

Leek vichyssoise with Kaffir lime leaves

This can be served hot or cold but if you're going for cold, thin it down with a little extra stock.

SERVES 4
60 g/2 oz butter
1 small onion, chopped
4 large leeks, trimmed and chopped
3 garlic cloves, peeled
1 large potato, roughly chopped
pinch of freshly grated nutmeg
800 ml/1⅓ pints vegetable stock made with ½ teaspoon bouillon powder
4 Kaffir lime leaves, crushed but not broken up
1 tablespoon double cream
salt and white pepper

Melt the butter in a heavy-bottomed saucepan. Add the onion, leeks and garlic and sweat until translucent.

Add the potato, nutmeg and a little of the stock. Cook quite fast for 5 minutes, then add the rest of the stock and the lime leaves and simmer for a further 10 minutes or so until the potato is tender right through.

Remove the lime leaves and purée in a blender until smooth. Return to the heat for a moment while you stir in the cream. Season with salt and white pepper and serve with crusty, warm French bread.

Carrot and almond soup

A quick glance at the ingredients may make you think: 'Is that it? Bit simple, isn't it?'
Yes, it is. And in my book, not bland but delicate. So delicate, I have to be in a particularly
sensitive mood for it. (Just as there are tomato-soup-and-a-wedge-of-Brie moments,
in my home there are carrot soup moments.) Even the parsley is only a reluctant addition
and I wouldn't usually bother. I want this silky smooth and as light as can be on the palate
and on the tummy. So no coriander for me this time please, and certainly no orange –
my lip curls when I remember that late 80s combo, Moroccan carrot and orange salad
notwithstanding.

SERVES 2
1 tablespoon sunflower oil
1 small onion, roughly diced
375 g/13 oz carrots, peeled and roughly chopped
1 garlic clove, peeled and left whole
400 ml/14 fl oz vegetable stock, made with ½ teaspoon bouillon powder
30 g/1 oz ground almonds
sea salt and freshly ground black pepper
1 tablespoon finely chopped fresh parsley
dash of tamari (optional)

Heat the oil in a saucepan and fry the onion until translucent. Add the carrots, the garlic
clove and about 3 tablespoons of stock. Simmer for a minute or two.

Meanwhile, in a small bowl, stir 3 tablespoons of the stock into the ground almonds to
form a cream.

Add the rest of the stock to the carrots and simmer until the carrots are soft. Stir in the
almond cream and purée in a blender until absolutely smooth. Add a little more stock to
adjust the consistency if necessary.

Season with salt and pepper, garnish with the parsley, a swirl of tamari if you must, and
serve with a warmed, lightly buttered baguette.

Cream of fennel soup with Pernod

The mild anise taste of slowly cooked fennel is accentuated by the Pernod. I sometimes add a tablespoon or two of ground almond to the fennel just before blending, which makes it somewhat more substantial. Try it either way.

SERVES 4

2 tablespoons groundnut oil or 30 g/1oz butter
1 shallot, finely chopped
3 large fennel bulbs, trimmed, roughly chopped but with the tough stalks in one piece and trimmed fronds reserved
1.75 litres/2¾ pints vegetable stock, made with 1½ teaspoons bouillon powder
2 garlic cloves, peeled and left whole
salt and white pepper
2 tablespoons double cream
2 tablespoons Pernod

Heat the oil or butter in a heavy-bottomed saucepan. Add the shallot and fennel, including the tough stalks, and cook slowly until softened, about 10 minutes.

Add the stock and garlic and season with salt and pepper. Cook for another 15 minutes.

Fish out the tough stalks and discard. Purée the soup in a blender until smooth.

Return to the heat for a moment while you stir in the cream and Pernod. Serve in individual bowls and garnish with the finest of the reserved fennel fronds.

Broad bean soup
with sun-dried tomatoes, tapenade and yoghurt

This is not the first time that cumin and paprika turn up in conjunction with broad beans in this book but as my assistant, Annabel, said when I showed it to her, 'Well, I would never have thought of it and it's delicious so please put it in.' So I have.

SERVES 2–4
1 tablespoon olive oil
1 onion, finely chopped
4 garlic cloves, crushed
1½ tablespoons ground cumin
1.5 litres/2½ pints hot vegetable stock, made with 3 teaspoons bouillon powder
1 kg/2 lb 4 oz frozen broad beans
1½ teaspoons tamari
good dash of Tabasco sauce
sea salt and freshly ground black pepper

to serve
4 whole sun-dried tomatoes in olive oil, snipped with scissors into small pieces
4 dessertspoons black olive tapenade or 6 black olives, roughly chopped
4 tablespoons Greek yoghurt
4 small sprigs of basil

Heat the olive oil in a heavy-bottomed saucepan. Add the onion and garlic and sweat until translucent.

Add the cumin and a tablespoon of stock and simmer for a few minutes, stirring constantly to stop the spices burning and darkening too much.

Add the broad beans and the rest of the stock, bring to the boil and cook for 8–12 minutes, until tender.

Purée in a blender until smooth – you can reserve a few whole broad beans to put back in after blending if you like. Return to the saucepan to heat through and stir in the tamari, Tabasco and salt and pepper to taste.

Serve in bowls, garnished with 1 snipped sun-dried tomato per person, a little black olive tapenade or chopped black olives, a spoonful of Greek yoghurt and a small sprig of basil. You can have extra olive oil handy if you wish and some warmed Arabic or other flat bread too, perhaps with a block of feta cheese to eat with it.

Sweet potato and tamarind soup

When I was a child, growing up in Casablanca, a winter (yes, there are winters in Casa) after-school snack was hot baked sweet potato. We would hold the potatoes in a napkin, cut them down the middle and eat the steaming hot, fluffy insides with a teaspoon. No salt, no pepper, no nothing. Frankly, I think this is as much as anyone ever really needs from a sweet potato and I suggest you try it. You and your children and your children's children. But of course, since I love them so much, there are several recipes for sweet potatoes in this book, including this easy and delicious soup.

SERVES 4
2 tablespoons olive oil
1 red onion, diced
4 garlic cloves, crushed
4 sweet potatoes, peeled and chopped
1 litre/1¾ pints vegetable stock, made with 1 teaspoon bouillon powder
1 tablespoon tamari
2 cm/1 inch piece of ginger, grated and squeezed, and the resulting liquid reserved
dash of Tabasco sauce
1–2 tablespoons tamarind paste
sea salt and freshly ground black pepper

Heat the oil in a saucepan, add the onion and garlic and sweat for 5 minutes.

Add the sweet potatoes and sauté for a further 5 minutes. Add the stock and simmer, covered, until tender, about 10 minutes.

Stir in the tamari, ginger juice, Tabasco and 1 tablespoon of tamarind paste, season with salt and pepper and blend until smooth.

Serve in bowls with a little extra tamarind paste swirled into each.

Butternut squash soup
with mango chutney and coriander pesto

As a way of putting a great soup, not to mention casserole, together in the briefest of time, pressure cookers take no beating. It helps to start and finish the dish off-pressure but they cut out all the slow bits in between. Make sure that the butternut flesh is bright orange. If you're landed with an insipid-looking one, add a chopped carrot to it. This recipe would also work well with pumpkin.

SERVES 4
3 tablespoons olive oil
1 onion, diced
3 garlic cloves, finely chopped
1 large butternut squash, peeled, seeds removed and cut into small chunks
800 ml/1⅓ pints hot vegetable stock, made with 1 teaspoon bouillon powder
1 teaspoon tamari
dash of Tabasco sauce
juice of half a lime
sea salt and freshly ground black pepper
1 tablespoon mango chutney
3 tablespoons coriander pesto (page 15)
a few sprigs of fresh coriander, torn

Heat the olive oil in a heavy-bottomed saucepan or pressure cooker. Fry the onion and garlic until translucent.

Add the butternut squash and fry until it just begins to speckle with brown and to soften a little, stirring pretty much constantly and slowly adding a couple of ladlefuls of stock to prevent it from sticking to the pan. Keep adjusting the heat from high to low and back again for about 5 minutes, until all the liquid is absorbed or evaporated.

Add the rest of the stock and cover with the pressure cooker lid. Bring to the boil, then reduce the heat and allow to simmer for 10 minutes. If you are not using a pressure cooker you will need to simmer for a little longer, until the butternut squash is tender. Remove from the heat.

Once the pressure has gone down, take the lid off and purée in a blender until smooth. Add the tamari, Tabasco, lime juice and salt and pepper to taste.

Serve in bowls and garnish with mango chutney, coriander pesto and a few shreds of fresh coriander.

Cream of petits pois

I made this one Christmas Eve, minutes before my guests were due to arrive. The soup was made and (which is rare) the blender washed and put away before the doorbell rang. There is enough starch in the peas to not even require a potato, but if you want to make this for lunch, I suggest you allow a small potato per person. Peel it and dice it, then sauté in olive oil until golden and serve separately for people to add to the soup. And Parmesan, shaved or grated, never goes amiss.

SERVES 4
30 g/1 oz butter
3 shallots, chopped
2 garlic cloves, crushed
375 g/13 oz frozen petits pois
700 ml/1¼ pints hot vegetable stock, made with 2 teaspoons bouillon powder
3 tablespoons double cream
sea salt and freshly ground black pepper
30 g/1 oz Parmesan, grated

Melt the butter in a saucepan. Add the shallots and garlic and sweat until translucent.

Add the frozen petits pois, cover with the hot stock and cook over a gentle heat for about 10 minutes.

When the peas are tender, blend until smooth. Return to the heat and stir in the cream. Season to taste with salt and pepper and serve with Parmesan to stir in.

Harira (chickpea soup) with harissa

This is the soup that Arabs famously break the fast of Ramadan with. When I was a child, I shared their mounting excitement (though not their hunger) as the aromas of the soup filled the house all afternoon and I absolutely loved the soup when it was finally ready. My mother tells me that sometimes dried broad beans would also go into it, and a huge piece of the stuff you probably don't eat any more if you're reading this. I don't need it and neither does the soup. To be able to make it in little more than 20 minutes is a modern development I am not going to complain about.

You'll have time while the soup cooks to put together a simple salad or two. How about a Moroccan grated carrot salad with some freshly squeezed orange juice and chopped-up orange, a little lemon juice and a touch of sugar, or some beetroot, thinly sliced and sprinkled with a little very finely minced onion and freshly ground cumin? You'll also have time to fry some flour tortillas (page 76); I defy you to need more.

SERVES 4
2 tablespoons olive oil, plus extra for serving
1 onion, roughly chopped
3 garlic cloves, finely sliced
1 stick of celery (optional)
2 teaspoons ground cumin
3 x 400 g/14 oz cans chickpeas, liquid included
generous pinch of saffron strands
1 dark vegetable stock cube
400 g/14 oz tomatoes, deseeded and roughly chopped
half a large bunch of coriander, chopped
juice of half a lemon
dash of Tabasco
sea salt and freshly ground black pepper

Heat the olive oil in a large saucepan and fry the onion until browned. Add the garlic, the celery if using, and the cumin and fry for another minute.

Add one can of chickpeas and the saffron, crumble in the stock cube and heat until bubbling gently, stirring to dissolve the stock cube – about 5 minutes.

Add the remaining chickpeas with all their liquid, together with an extra 250 ml/8 fl oz of water. Leave on a gentle heat to cook for 15 minutes or so.

Add the chopped tomatoes and – a minute later – half the coriander, the lemon juice, Tabasco, salt and pepper. Stir for a minute, then remove from the heat.

Transfer to a warmed soup tureen or individual bowls and garnish with the rest of the coriander and a swirl of olive oil if you wish.

Miso noodle soup with tempura

Japanese and Chinese noodle soups, South-east Asian laksas, all make great fast and healthy meals. The sheer volume of liquid makes you feel inordinately full, and the seasonings are surprisingly delicate and fragrant. They are all bulked out with noodles, so you really can make a meal out of them. The large, canteen-style, modern Chinese restaurants, feeding the 5,000 so to speak, have made much of them on their menus so you can be sure that they are easy to execute, especially when broken down into stages. They epitomize the clean yet many layered tastes of the Far East and you can reflect that in the presentation by keeping back a little of each ingredient for garnish.

SERVES 2
about 400 ml/14 fl oz groundnut oil for deep frying
4 spring onions, finely sliced
6 garlic cloves, finely sliced
4 stalks of lemongrass, very finely sliced
2 small carrots, cut in half lengthways and thinly sliced into half moons
100 g/3½ oz baby corn, cut in half lengthways
250 g/9 oz shiitake mushrooms, sliced into 4 or more pieces
60 g/2 oz mangetout, topped and tailed
125 g/4 oz fine egg noodles
6 tablespoons pale miso
50 g/1½ oz ginger, grated and squeezed, and the resulting liquid reserved
1 bird's eye chilli, finely chopped
handful of fresh coriander, roughly chopped
juice of 1 lime
1½ teaspoons soft brown sugar
3 tablespoons ume su, a Japanese vinegar made from umeboshi plums (optional)
1 tablespoon tamari, plus extra for dipping
chilli sauce (page 62, optional)

tempura
½ red or yellow pepper, cut into 4 wide strips
1 courgette, sliced into diagonal slices about 1 cm/½ inch thick
1 small red onion, cut into rings

tempura batter
60 g/2 oz self-raising flour, sifted
good pinch of salt
100 ml/3½ fl oz lukewarm water
2 tablespoons sparkling water or lager
1 egg white, whisked to soft peaks

To make the tempura batter, mix together the flour, salt and water, both ordinary and sparkling (or lager), in a bowl and stir with a fork. Don't worry if lumps form – you'll see that there will be no nasty side effects when you fry it. Remember that once you add the egg white, the batter must be used immediately, so set it aside for now.

Bring a kettle of water to the boil. You will need it for the miso stock and you might need a little for cooking the vegetables.

Bring a large saucepan of salted water to the boil to cook the noodles in.

Heat the groundnut oil in a deep pan or wok for deep-frying the tempura and keep an eye on it.

Transfer 2 tablespoons of the groundnut oil into a large saucepan. Add the spring onions, garlic, lemongrass, carrots and baby corn, and finally the mushrooms and mangetout. Sauté for a minute, adding a tablespoon or two of the boiling water to prevent the vegetables from sticking to the bottom of the pan and to create steam, which helps them to cook.

Meanwhile, cook the noodles according to packet instructions.

Fold the whisked egg white into the tempura batter. Dip the prepared tempura vegetables into the batter and drop them carefully into the hot oil, just a few at a time or they won't cook quickly enough. When they rise to the surface, allow them to go golden and crispy and turn them using two forks so that they are done all over. Transfer immediately to a colander lined with kitchen paper.

While the tempura is frying, go back to the soup. Add 2 litres/3½ pints of boiling water to the stir-fried soup vegetables, together with the miso, and stir until it dissolves. Add the ginger juice, extracting as much liquid as you can, the chilli, coriander, lime juice, brown sugar and the ume su if using, and finally the tamari.

Drain the noodles and stir them into the hot vegetable broth. Bring it just to boiling point and immediately remove from the heat. Miso should not boil as this destroys all its famed healing properties.

Serve the broth in deep bowls. Place 3–4 pieces of tempura into each bowl and serve at once, with any remaining tempura on a separate plate with a little tamari and/or chilli sauce for dipping.

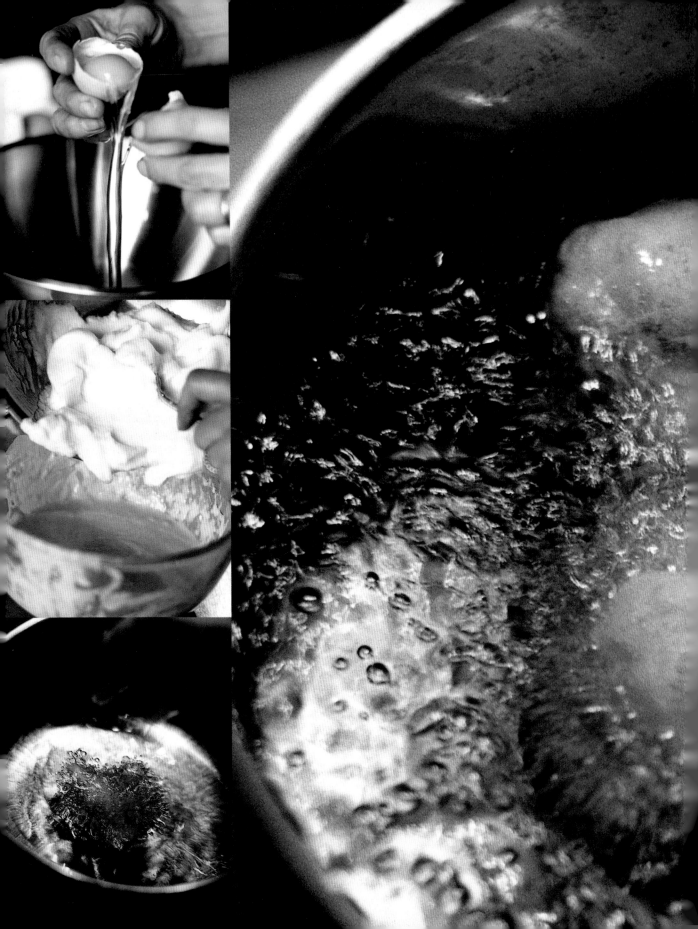

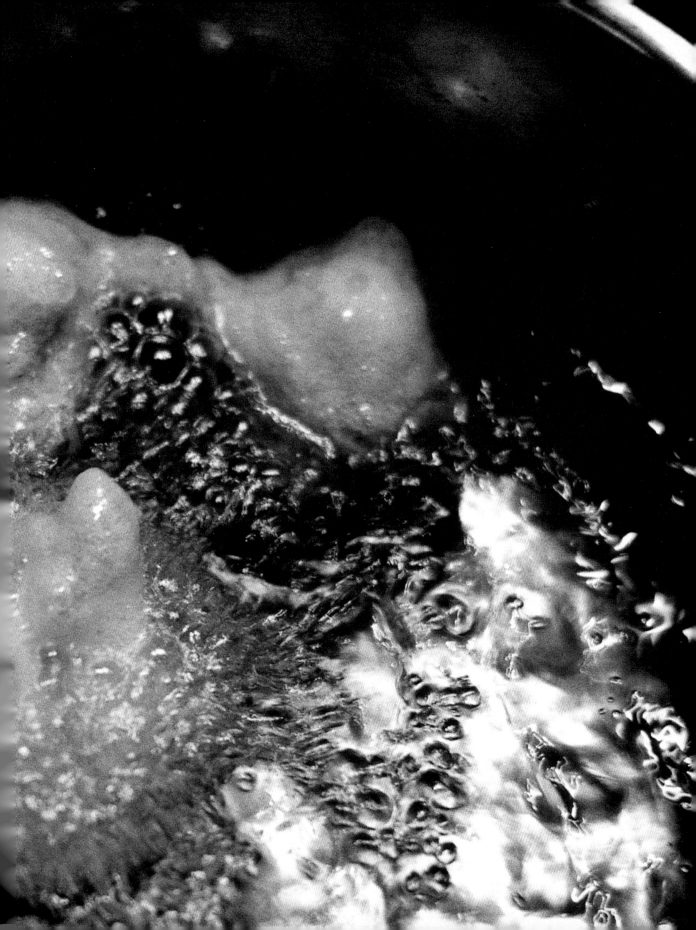

Coconut and spinach laksa with deep-fried tofu

SERVES 2
tempura batter (pages 46–47)
about 400 ml/14 fl oz groundnut oil for deep frying
2 garlic cloves, finely sliced
2 teaspoons Thai seven spice
60 g/2 oz ginger, grated and squeezed, and the resulting liquid reserved
2 stalks of lemongrass, very finely sliced
1 bird's eye chilli, very finely chopped
150 g/5 oz butternut squash, peeled and cut into 2 cm/1 inch cubes
400 ml/14 fl oz unsweetened coconut milk
200 ml/7 fl oz water or light vegetable stock, made with a pinch of bouillon powder
150 g/5 oz plain tofu, cut into 4 cm/2 inch cubes
small handful or 1 nest of fine egg noodles
60 g/2 oz baby spinach
1 teaspoon tamarind paste

to serve
small handful of coriander leaves, 1 lime, tamari

Prepare the tempura batter. Remember that once you add the egg whites the batter must be used immediately, so set it aside for now. Heat the groundnut oil in a wok or deep pan in anticipation of deep frying the tofu; keep an eye on it as you continue with the preparation.

To make the laksa, heat 1 tablespoon of the groundnut oil in a heavy-bottomed saucepan. Add the garlic, Thai seven spice, ginger juice, lemongrass and half the chilli. Cook for about 4–5 minutes. Add the butternut squash and sauté until just soft. Then add the coconut milk and half the water or stock and simmer gently for a few minutes.

Add the remaining water or stock and continue to simmer for about 6–7 minutes, until some of the butternut squash begins to dissolve, a process which you can accelerate by mashing some of the pieces with the back of a fork.

Meanwhile, finish the batter by folding in the egg whites. Dip the pieces of tofu into it and then drop carefully into the hot oil. Cook until golden brown all over. Transfer immediately to a colander lined with kitchen paper.

Finally, add the nest of noodles to the laksa and cook for 3 minutes. Reserving a few raw leaves for garnish, add the spinach and cook gently until wilted. Stir in the tamarind paste.

Serve in bowls with the remaining chilli, spinach leaves and several pieces of deep-fried tofu in each. Finish with a sprig or two of coriander and serve with half a lime and a little tamari. To enjoy the deep-fried tofu at its best, don't waste a moment before eating.

Thai stir fry

Quick to make because of the low maintenance needs of the chosen vegetables. Take care with the Chinese cabbage, however, that it cooks for the briefest time or it will weep uncontrollably. To turn this recipe into the famous – and even quicker – *pad thai*, omit all the vegetables except the beansprouts and spring onions and add a couple of eggs. Let them set for several seconds before adding the noodles, and stir well to combine them.

SERVES 4
150 ml/5 fl oz hot vegetable stock, made with ½ teaspoon bouillon powder
3 tablespoons groundnut oil
2 stalks of lemongrass
200 g/7 oz small broccoli florets
125 g/4 oz baby corn, cut in half lengthways
180 g/6 oz mangetout, topped and tailed
150 g/5 oz Chinese cabbage, coarsely shredded
4 spring onions, trimmed and sliced on the slant
6 Kaffir lime leaves
150 g/5 oz beansprouts (optional)

sauce
6 garlic cloves, roughly chopped
1 bird's eye chilli, finely chopped
7 cm/3 inch piece of fresh ginger, grated and squeezed, and the resulting
    liquid reserved
2 tablespoons soft brown sugar
2 tablespoons chopped fresh coriander
1 tablespoon tamarind paste
2 tablespoons peanuts, salted or unsalted

First make the sauce. Put all the ingredients (reserving a few peanuts for garnishing) in a blender or food processor and blitz to a rough paste. Transfer to a bowl and add about 90 ml/3 fl oz of the hot vegetable stock and 1 tablespoon of the oil. Stir and set aside.

Heat the remaining oil in a large frying pan or wok. Add the lemongrass and broccoli, stir. A minute later add the baby corn, then the mangetout, then the Chinese cabbage, spring onions and lime leaves. Stir-fry over high heat for 1–2 minutes. Add a couple of tablespoons of stock to the sizzling vegetables to loosen the juices if necessary.

Quickly stir in the beansprouts, if using, then remove from the heat, pour the sauce over and garnish with the reserved peanuts. Serve with plain rice or udon noodles, with tamari and chilli oil to season.

Shiitake, bok choy, spring onion and cashew stir fry with udon noodles

I used to wander into Soho's Chinatown and marvel at the Chinese greens. I would occasionally buy them and guess – not hard to do – how to cook them. Now several varieties are available in supermarkets. I've noticed that the supermarket packets often tell you to remove the stalks. I've never found this to be necessary.

SERVES 2–4
3 tablespoons groundnut oil
4 heads of bok choy, sliced in half lengthways
200 g/7 oz shiitake mushrooms, halved
1 bunch of spring onions, trimmed and sliced on the slant
30 g/1 oz cashew nuts, salted or toasted unsalted
few flecks of a finely chopped red chilli
few small sprigs of coriander (optional)

sauce
2 tablespoons tamari
2 tablespoons pale yellow bean paste
1 small bird's eye chilli, finely chopped
1 garlic clove, sliced
1 thumb of ginger, grated
1 teaspoon brown sugar
1 dessertspoon arrowroot

Mix all the sauce ingredients, excluding the arrowroot, together with 150 ml/5 fl oz of water and set aside.

Heat 2 tablespoons of the groundnut oil in a heavy-bottomed saucepan or wok. Add the bok choy and sauté for a couple of minutes until softened. Then add 2–3 tablespoons of the sauce, stirring and taking care that it does not burn. Add the mushrooms and cook for a minute or so on a fairly high heat, until they are soft and glistening, adding spoonfuls of the sauce until about half is used up. Add the spring onions, stirring until they just wilt.

Dissolve the arrowroot in the remaining sauce and add it to the pan, stirring quickly until the sauce is thickened and generously coating the vegetables. If cooking on a very high heat the pan may dry out a little. If so, add a drop or two of water. Remove from the heat and add the cashew nuts and a smattering of chilli, as well as the coriander if using.

Serve at once with some thick and slippery udon noodles (cooked according to packet instructions) or a bowl of basmati rice into which you have scrambled an egg and a chopped spring onion or two at the last minute.

Fab fritters and friends What's a little oil between friends? Most of these fritters are only shallow fried, and always in fresh, light oil (for good health, never ever re-use cooking oil). Everyone needs a little comfort food sometimes and nothing does it quite like crisp, golden, sizzling fried food.

Deep-fried cauliflower fritters
with caper mayonnaise

As children we often ate these served with a tomato sauce. I like them with the combined sharpness and richness of the caper mayonnaise. Capers packed in salt look great but I can't help preferring the sharper, less fattened ones of my childhood, preserved in very unfashionable brine.

SERVES 4
1 large cauliflower, broken into florets
at least 1 litre/1¾ pints groundnut oil for deep frying
plain white flour for coating
3 large eggs, beaten
sea salt

caper mayonnaise
50 g/1½ oz capers, packed in salt or brine, washed or drained
100 g/3½ oz good-quality mayonnaise

Mix the capers with the mayonnaise and put to one side.

Bring a large saucepan of salted water to the boil, drop in the cauliflower florets and cook until al dente. Drain very well.

Heat the oil in a deep-frying pan or deep saucepan until very hot, then reduce the heat.

Meanwhile, coat the florets first in the flour, then in the beaten egg. Drop them into the hot oil – you may have to do this in batches – and cook until they are golden brown all over, turning them with two forks.

Transfer to a colander lined with a double layer of kitchen paper. Salt immediately and serve at once with the caper mayonnaise.

Potato rosti
with wilted spinach, mushrooms and a poached egg

I once lived in Zurich for six months. There, with quite a lot of help from my friends, I ran the kitchen of a 170-seater vegetarian restaurant. When I tell you that fresh morels and white truffles appeared on the menu, that there was an Italian chef, assisted by a couple of deft Japanese sushi chefs, you will see that this was no ordinary vegetarian restaurant. Anyway, it was there that I learned to make rosti – perfect Sunday brunch material.

SERVES 2–4
500 g/1 lb 2 oz waxy potatoes
4 tablespoons butter
half an onion, finely chopped
sea salt and freshly ground black pepper
groundnut oil for frying
30 g/1 oz dried porcini mushrooms, soaked in a little boiling water with a dash of tamari or
    150 g/5 oz chestnut mushrooms, thickly sliced
1–2 tablespoons double cream
200 g/7 oz baby spinach
pinch of freshly grated nutmeg
4 large free range eggs

Place the potatoes, skin and all, in a saucepan of salted water. Parboil for 10 minutes. Drain and, when cool enough to handle, peel and grate. Heat 2 tablespoons of the butter in a small frying pan and gently sweat the onion until golden. Add to the grated potato, together with some salt and pepper.

Heat a little oil in a nonstick or cast-iron frying pan. Spread the potato mixture in the pan, flattening it with a spatula, and fry on a medium heat until it is a deep golden brown. Slide out onto a plate, then turn over and return to the pan to cook the other side. Turn out and cut into four. Or make four individual rosti in exactly the same way.

Sauté the mushrooms in 1 tablespoon of butter for a couple of minutes and add a dash of double cream. Meanwhile, wilt the spinach in a hot pan with the rest of the butter, some pepper and a little nutmeg to taste, adding salt only at the end as it draws out so much of the juice otherwise. Squeeze out the excess liquid anyway and set aside.

Poach the eggs one at a time. I put about 4 cm/2 inches of water in a small pan, bring it to the boil, then reduce the heat to the merest simmer. I then drop the egg into the water and let it sit there for a minute or so, until the white is firm and a very fine film has formed over the yolk. Then I use a fish slice to gently lift and drain it.

Serve the components separately or pile up in the manner of eggs Florentine.

Aubergine, mozzarella and sun-dried tomato stacks

Smoked mozzarella balls tend to be bigger, heavier and of course drier and easier to slice than the normal milky white version. As well as the watercress pesto, I love these served with a watercress salad too. Serve about five stacks per person or three as a starter.

SERVES 4–6
3 large free range eggs
sea salt and freshly ground black pepper
1–2 aubergines, cut into 10–15 slices each, ½ cm/¼ inch thick
a little olive oil and lemon juice
6 tablespoons watercress pesto (page 15)
20–30 pieces sun-dried tomatoes in oil
20–30 basil leaves, left whole
20–30 black olives, stoned
2–3 mozzarella balls (150 g/5 oz each), smoked if possible, sliced into 10 slices each
100 ml/3½ oz olive oil for frying
1 lemon, cut into wedges

Beat the eggs, season with a little salt and pepper and set aside. Lightly salt the aubergines, then brush lightly with olive oil and lemon juice.

Prepare the stacks: one slice of aubergine, spread with a little pesto, followed by a piece of sun-dried tomato, a basil leaf, then a black olive or two, and a slice of mozzarella.

Heat the oil in a frying pan.

Holding them together, dip each stack into the beaten egg, then fry on both sides until golden, starting with the aubergine side and taking a little longer with it than with the cheese side. Just before turning the stack over onto the cheese side, spoon over a little extra beaten egg. These should take about 1 minute on each side.

Transfer to a plate lined with kitchen paper. Sprinkle with salt and any remaining watercress pesto. Serve at once, cheese side up, with lemon wedges to squeeze over the fritters. Don't forget the watercress, just lightly dressed with olive oil and a little balsamic vinegar.

Moroccan potato pastelles

To make more of a meal of these, serve with grilled pepper strips seasoned with a little olive oil, crushed garlic, salt and pepper; a salad of finely sliced peeled cucumber dressed with a little vinaigrette; and a salad of beetroot with a dash of vinegar, a generous pinch of ground cumin and a smattering of very finely minced onion. A good fresh tomato sauce goes very well, as does a little harissa or chermoula (page 17).

MAKES 10 PASTELLES
1 kg/2 lb 4 oz potatoes, red-skinned if possible, peeled and cut into chunks
4 large eggs, beaten
sea salt and freshly ground black pepper
pinch of freshly grated nutmeg
2 tablespoons olive oil
groundnut oil for frying

filling
60 g/2 oz mushrooms, sliced and sautéed in a little olive oil with 1 teaspoon tamari
90 g/3 oz spinach, tossed in a hot pan until wilted, then drained and chopped
pinch of freshly grated nutmeg
sea salt and freshly ground black pepper
1 hard-boiled egg, peeled and chopped
1 tablespoon fresh herbs (parsley, coriander, basil, chives or any combination of these)
1 garlic clove, crushed
1 spring onion or shallot, finely chopped
30 g/1 oz mature Cheddar or other strong cheese, grated

Place the potatoes in a large saucepan of salted water and bring to the boil, then simmer until tender and drain thoroughly. Mash until smooth with a potato masher or by passing through a mouli légumes. Meanwhile, prepare the filling ingredients, mix well and season with salt and pepper.

Add two of the beaten eggs to the mashed potato, then the salt, pepper and nutmeg to taste. Work with your hand or a fork until well amalgamated.

Divide the potato purée into 10 even-sized lumps, about 4 cm/2 inches in diameter. Lightly oil your hands with olive oil and flatten a lump between the palms of your hands. Place a little of the filling in the centre, then bring the potato around it, making sure that the filling is well sealed in. Dip the pastelles in the rest of the beaten egg.

Heat the groundnut oil in a frying pan and fry the pastelles in two batches until they are crisp and golden. Transfer to a plate lined with kitchen paper. Sprinkle with salt and serve at once.

Scotch pancakes (choose your topping)

SERVES 4–6 (about 25 pancakes)
350 g/12 oz plain flour, sifted
3 teaspoons baking powder
pinch of salt
½ teaspoon soft brown sugar
2 eggs
350 ml/12 fl oz milk
75 g/2½ oz butter, melted
groundnut oil for frying

Sift the flour with the baking powder and salt into a bowl, add the sugar, and make a well in the centre.

Beat the eggs and then whisk in the milk and melted butter. Pour into the centre of the well of flour and whisk until the batter is smooth, adding a little more milk if necessary.

Heat a heavy-bottomed frying pan and wipe with a little groundnut oil. Drop spoonfuls of the batter onto the hot pan. When golden, flip over and cook the other side.

Serve with any or several of these:
black olive tapenade
sun-dried tomato purée
crème fraîche or garlic yoghurt
quick guacamole, made by blending or mashing the flesh of a ripe avocado with a tablespoon of olive oil, one of water, some sea salt, freshly ground black pepper and a crushed garlic clove
griddled red peppers
pesto
cottage cheese
quick houmous, made by blending a can of drained chickpeas with 4 tablespoons olive oil, a crushed garlic clove, a little ground cumin, a tablespoon of tahini and 2 tablespoons of the chickpea liquid

Corn fritters with avocado and mango salsa

These are firmer and better textured with corn straight from the cob. If you have to use frozen then just add a little more flour and expect the fritters to spit at you as they cook. If, on the other hand, the fritters seem a bit dry because your corn is so young that it releases very little juice, you may need to add a tablespoon of water to the mix.

SERVES 2–4 (about 12 fritters)
3 ears of corn, to yield about 225 g/8 oz kernels in total
5 tablespoons double cream
3 tablespoons plain flour
½ teaspoon baking powder
½ teaspoon brown sugar
1 tablespoon chopped fresh coriander, plus a few sprigs to garnish (optional)
small piece of red chilli, diced
sea salt and freshly ground black pepper
light olive oil for frying
1–2 perfectly ripe avocados (allowing half an avocado per person), sliced horizontally
juice of 1 lime

salsa
1 tablespoon olive oil
half a small red onion, very finely chopped
1 mango, ripe but not too soft, peeled and cut into small cubes
small bunch of coriander, chopped
small piece of red chilli, chopped very fine
2 cm/1 inch piece of ginger, grated and squeezed, and the resulting liquid reserved
dash of Tabasco sauce

to serve
1 tablespoon chilli sauce (from a jar), loosened with 4 tablespoons groundnut or light
   olive oil, a dash of Tabasco and a pinch of sugar

First make the salsa. In a serving bowl, mix together the olive oil, onion, mango, coriander, chilli, ginger juice and Tabasco. Or, for a warm topping, heat the oil in a small saucepan and sauté the onion until translucent. Add the mango and stir gently for a minute to warm through, then add the remaining ingredients. Stir quickly and remove from the heat.

To make the fritters, cut the corn from the cob with a sharp knife. Place the kernels and juice, if any, in a bowl. Add the cream, flour, baking powder, sugar, coriander, chilli, salt and pepper and mix well.

Heat a couple of tablespoons of oil in a griddle or shallow frying pan. Drop tablespoonfuls of the corn mixture into the pan and flatten them with the back of a spoon. Fry until golden, about 4 minutes on each side or until the corn starts to pop and spit. Transfer immediately to a large plate lined with kitchen paper and sprinkle with a little salt. Keep warm in the oven if necessary until you're ready to serve.

To serve, allow at least three fritters per person and place three half-moon slices of avocado on each fritter, then squeeze a little lime juice over each portion. Top with a little of the mango salsa and a few drops of the chilli sauce. The fritters can be stacked up with the fillings in between, if you are into that sort of thing, or take the ingredients to the table in separate dishes and allow for a bit of DIY. Garnish with sprigs of coriander if you like. Whatever, the fritters must be hot and crisp.

Tempura

SERVES 4

900 ml/1½ pints groundnut or sunflower oil for deep frying
1 red pepper, deseeded and pith removed, cut into 8 long strips
1 yellow pepper, deseeded and pith removed, cut into 8 long strips
1 large courgette, sliced on the slant, about ½ cm/¼ inch thick
8 chestnut mushrooms, left whole
1 red onion, cut into rings about ¼ cm/⅛ inch thick
90 g/3 oz green beans, topped and tailed and lightly blanched (5 minutes in boiling
   water and then refreshed in cold water)
100 g/3½ oz broccoli florets, about 4 cm/2 inches in diameter
100 g/3½ oz cauliflower florets, about 4 cm/2 inches in diameter

tempura batter
100 g/3½ oz self-raising flour, sifted
good pinch of salt
200 ml/7 fl oz lukewarm water
5 tablespoons sparkling water or lager
2 egg whites, whisked to soft peaks

to serve
tamari
chilli sauce (page 62)

Heat the oil in a deep pan or wok.

To make the batter, mix together the flour, salt and water, both ordinary and sparkling (or lager), in a bowl and stir with a fork. Don't worry if lumps form – they will disappear when you fry the tempura. Fold in the whisked egg whites.

Dip the vegetable pieces into the batter and drop them carefully into the hot oil, just a few at a time or they won't cook quickly enough. When they rise to the surface, allow them to go golden and crispy and turn them using two forks so that they are done all over. Transfer immediately to a colander lined with kitchen paper.

Serve with little bowls of tamari and chilli sauce for dipping or some mayonnaise with plenty of crushed garlic.

Risotto fritters

Use any leftover cooked risotto – for example, if you follow a recipe for six and serve four – you will have enough left over to make fritters for two as a main course or four as an appetizer.

SERVES 2–4

Shape the cold risotto in the palm of your hands into rounded balls about 7 cm/3 inches in diameter. You could, if you like, put a little piece of Fontina, Taleggio, mozzarella or some other cheese or a knob of garlic butter into the centre of the patty, shaping the rice around it.

Coat the rice balls lightly in a little sifted flour and then some beaten egg and shallow fry in a little heated groundnut oil until golden. Immediately sprinkle with salt and serve hot.

Serve with any of these:
grilled or griddled vegetables, either on the side or placed on top
olive purée – black or green – or sun-dried tomato purée
wilted spinach and fried mushrooms
anything else that you might serve with rosti, pancakes or blinis

Instead of fritters, you could make a kind of frittata by heating a little olive oil in a frying pan – nonstick makes it very easy – adding the cold risotto, then pouring 3–4 beaten eggs into the rice and cooking gently until set and browned underneath. Slide out onto a plate, then turn over back into the pan and fry on the other side until golden brown. Serve hot from the pan.

Black-eyed bean burgers

Burger has become almost a dirty word, not to mention a pretty filthy product, and the vegetarian attempts are of the same ilk – too greasy, too bland, too dead. These are simple but clean-tasting and fresh and they'll take all manner of side kicks to set them off: relishes, mustard, a good strong caper mayonnaise, onion (raw or browned), even some tomato ketchup – the works.

SERVES 2–4
400 g/14 oz can black-eyed beans, drained
1 shallot, finely chopped
1 spring onion, finely sliced
1 garlic clove, crushed
2 tablespoons chopped fresh coriander
6 chestnut mushrooms, thickly sliced and sautéed in a little olive oil
dash of tamari
dash of Tabasco sauce
sea salt and freshly ground black pepper
2–3 tablespoons groundnut oil

Lightly mash the beans and mix all the ingredients except the oil together and set aside while you prepare your accompaniments: caper mayonnaise (page 56); green salad, rocket, baby spinach or watercress; slices of tomato; paper-thin slices of raw red onion or fried onions.

Heat the groundnut oil in a frying pan.

Shape the bean mixture with the palms of your hand into two large or four medium burgers. Fry on one side until brown and crisp. Then, using a large fish slice, carefully turn over and fry the other side.

Serve in warmed ciabatta or crusty rolls, with your chosen salad and accompaniments.

Warm salads In a hurry, I am more likely to turn to warm salads than to anything else. The colours, textures and tastes make me feel I am eating something altogether grander than a salad, yet mopping up the dressing with warm bread is one of the most basic, homely, comforting things I can think of.

Ful medames with tahini spinach

This kind of food is my ground, the place I return to most easily. For a time it was almost a secret. I felt it wasn't sophisticated, impressive or difficult enough; on top of which, vegetarian food so often turned to so-called ethnic cuisines with heavy-handed results. I wanted my cooking to be light, colourful, refined. And I think my mother felt the same: the Moroccan touch infused an otherwise very French kitchen like a distant memory.

SERVES 4
2 x 400g/14 oz cans ful medames (page 12), liquid included
1 garlic clove, finely sliced
1 tablespoon chopped fresh parsley
2 tablespoons olive oil
½ teaspoon ground cumin
lemon juice to taste

tahini spinach
250 g/9 oz spinach, washed
1 garlic clove, crushed
pinch of freshly grated nutmeg
sea salt and freshly ground black pepper
1 tablespoon light tahini (or Greek yoghurt, if you prefer)
1 tablespoon pine nuts

to serve
4 pitta breads
2 teaspoons extra virgin olive oil
½ teaspoon cumin seeds
Greek yoghurt
preserved or fresh lemon

Preheat the oven to 200°C/400°F/gas 6. Mix all the ful medames ingredients together in a colourful bowl and set aside.

Toss the washed spinach in a hot pan until it wilts, then squeeze out all excess liquid. Season with the garlic, nutmeg, salt and pepper and stir in the tahini or Greek yoghurt.

Place the pitta breads on a baking sheet and brush with the olive oil and cumin seeds. Put them in the hot oven for 5–10 minutes, with the pine nuts on the side. When the pine nuts are lightly toasted, sprinkle them over the spinach. Serve immediately, with the pitta bread and a bowl of Greek yoghurt, preserved lemon or simply some lemon wedges.

Warm cauliflower
with green olives, feta and preserved lemon

This is certainly a different take on cauliflower and cheese – much quicker, aromatic and more cross-seasonal than the usual. I use good-quality stoned green olives which are quite mild, but you could use Middle Eastern cracked ones if you like.

SERVES 2–4
4 tablespoons olive oil
1 perfectly white cauliflower, leaves removed, broken into florets
½–1 teaspoon cumin seeds
1 tablespoon preserved lemon dressing (page 17) or about ¼ of a preserved lemon, chopped finely
60 g/2 oz green olives
small pinch of cayenne pepper
sea salt
30 g/1 oz feta cheese

Heat a little less than half the olive oil in a large sauté pan. Add the cauliflower florets and sauté until evenly browned and softened but still with a little crunch. This will take 8–10 minutes.

Add the cumin seeds and sauté for a further 30 seconds or so. Transfer to a bowl and mix with the preserved lemon, olives, cayenne pepper and salt. Despite the feta, the cauliflower can handle a fair amount of salt.

Pour over the remaining olive oil and crumble the feta on top. Serve as soon as you can with any warmed Middle Eastern bread.

Seared green beans with potatoes, mushrooms and six-minute eggs

This is my version of a salade niçoise; I think it bears enough similarity to warrant the comparison. Open a window while you griddle the vegetables – it can get very smoky.

SERVES 4
2 large flat open cap mushrooms, or 3 portobello mushrooms, thickly sliced
2 teaspoons tamari
300 g/11 oz green beans, topped and tailed
500 g/1 lb 2 oz new potatoes, preferably waxy, cut in half
light olive oil for shallow frying
4 large free range eggs
20 pieces of slow-roasted tomato (page 16)
sea salt and freshly ground black pepper

dressing
6 tablespoons olive oil
1½ tablespoons balsamic vinegar
4 garlic cloves, crushed
2 teaspoons English mustard

Mix all the ingredients for the dressing, set aside. Baste the mushrooms with the tamari.

Bring a saucepan of salted water to the boil and blanch the green beans for 5 minutes. Scoop out the beans with a slotted spoon, refresh under cold running water, drain well and set aside. In the same pan, boil the potatoes until cooked. Drain.

Heat a griddle pan. Baste the mushrooms and beans lightly in the dressing. Cook the mushrooms on the hot griddle pan until lightly charred, then remove and cook the beans in the same way. Set aside.

Now wipe the pan clean with a piece of kitchen paper, then add a couple of tablespoons of oil to the pan. Sauté the potatoes until golden and charred in places.

Meanwhile, place the eggs in a saucepan of cold water and bring to the boil. Boil for exactly 6 minutes from the moment it reaches boiling point. The whites should be completely set but the yolks still runny. Refresh under a cold tap while you shell very carefully.

To serve, mix the green beans, mushrooms, tomatoes and potatoes together with the remaining dressing. Cut the eggs in half and put on top, then season with salt and pepper to taste. Serve immediately.

Spicy warm potato salad with a Moorish influence

Serve this as part of a mezze platter of quickly prepared things such as the tahini spinach (page 72), slow-roasted tomatoes (page 16), a rocket or other green salad, Smoked aubergines (page 24) or just a plate of grilled peppers, doused in lemon juice, olive oil and crushed garlic. There are lots of possibilities. You need a floury potato such as King Edward, all the better to absorb the dressing with. Serve warm, with a slab of feta cheese, which you cut into thin morsels to place on top of each potato slice. Serve with tiny dabs of harissa for a potato salad that breaks the usual mould.

SERVES 2
2 large potatoes, peeled and cut into slices about 1 cm/½ inch thick
3 tablespoons olive oil, quite green and rough
1 tablespoon coriander, chopped
sea salt and freshly ground black pepper
pinch of paprika
½ teaspoon cumin seeds

to serve
olive oil for frying
2 or more flour tortillas
feta cheese
harissa

Boil the potatoes in plenty of salted water until they are very soft: almost, but not quite, to breaking point. Drain well.

Put them in a bowl and pour over the olive oil, add the coriander and season with salt and pepper. Mix very gently.

Lay the potato slices flat on a plate and pour the olive oil dressing they were just mixed in on top. Sprinkle with paprika.

Toast the cumin seeds for a few seconds in a dry frying pan and let them be your finishing touch.

To serve, make a quick imitation of a real Arabic bread – melawah – that is difficult to find and notoriously difficult to make (or so I have always been told). Heat a little olive oil in a frying pan and fry the tortillas for about 30 seconds on either side. Serve with the feta cheese and harissa.

Roasted beetroots with halloumi and green beans

If you can find tiny bunched beetroots, still with their delicious tops on, that would be great (add the cleaned leaves, very lightly blanched if you like, to the salad at the end). If you can't, then use unvinegared baby beetroots or larger ones cut into pieces. Grill them with the halloumi while it reaches its part-molten, part-crisp, golden ideal. You could replace the green beans with purple sprouting broccoli in its precious short season.

SERVES 2
275 g/10 oz baby beetroots, cooked, or 350 g/12 oz bunched baby beetroots, cut in half
   if necessary
125 g/4 oz halloumi cheese, cut into finger-size strips
3 tablespoons olive oil
½ teaspoon cumin seeds, lightly toasted
125 g/4 oz green beans, topped and tailed
1 teaspoon balsamic vinegar
1 tablespoon crème fraîche or Greek yoghurt (optional)
dash of Tabasco sauce
sea salt and freshly ground black pepper

Preheat the grill. Place the baby beetroots and halloumi on a metal (conducts the heat better) baking sheet. Baste with 2 tablespoons of the olive oil and grill for about 5 minutes, turning over so that the halloumi is golden and crisp on the outside and the beetroots are wrinkled without and tender within. Put the cumin seeds alongside and remove as soon as they start to darken.

Meanwhile, bring a pan of water to the boil. Blanch the green beans until tender, refresh under cold running water and set aside.

Mix the remaining ingredients together, including the crème fraîche or Greek yoghurt if using. Add the beetroots, green beans and halloumi and mix gently. Sprinkle the cumin seeds on top. Serve at once with chunks of warm bread.

Chickpea, lemon and herb salad
with tomatoes and grilled halloumi

This takes only minutes to prepare, but succeeds in being rustic and elegant at the same time. Supermarket rocket will do here, of course, and some are even selling wild now, but even if you only have a windowbox, rocket is something you can grow with minimal effort.

SERVES 2–4
2 x 400 g/14 oz cans chickpeas, drained
1 tablespoon fresh lemon juice
2 tablespoons each of parsley and coriander, chopped
2 tablespoons extra virgin olive oil, plus a little more for basting the cheese
1 garlic clove, crushed
dash of tamari
dash of Tabasco sauce
sea salt and freshly ground black pepper
200 g/7 oz halloumi cheese
100 g/3½ oz wild rocket or baby spinach leaves
12 cherry tomatoes (preferably organic), cut in half, or 24 pieces of slow-roasted tomato
    quarters (page 16)
100 g/3½ oz black olives

Preheat your grill or a griddle pan.

In a bowl, mix the chickpeas with the lemon juice, parsley and coriander, olive oil, garlic, tamari, Tabasco and salt and pepper to taste. Set aside.

Cut the halloumi into ½ cm/¼ inch thick slices. Baste with a little olive oil, then grill or griddle for about 1 minute on each side, until it is golden brown.

Make a mound of rocket or spinach leaves on each plate. Divide the chickpea salad between the plates and garnish artfully with the tomatoes and olives. Top with the grilled halloumi, allowing about three slices per person. Drizzle any remaining dressing over the top and eat at once, with some warmed bread.

Red pepper, asparagus and courgettes
with butterbeans

Infinitely preferable are the Judion butterbeans in jars now available in most supermarkets, though needs must and canned ones will do. The dressing is more than enough, but it keeps well in the fridge for over a week. Gently warm to serve, loosened with a tablespoon or two of water. Remember too that it is very rich, so use sparingly.

SERVES 2–4
275 g/10 oz asparagus
1 courgette, topped and tailed, and cut lengthways into ½ cm/¼ inch ribbons
1 red pepper, deseeded and pith removed, cut into 8 strips
3 tablespoons light olive oil
1 tablespoon parsley, very finely chopped
200 g/7 oz cooked butterbeans, with a tablespoon of their liquid reserved
dash of Tabasco sauce

dressing
2 tablespoons extra virgin olive oil
6 tablespoons balsamic vinegar
1 tablespoon tamari
1 teaspoon brown sugar
3 garlic cloves, crushed
4 tablespoons Cointreau or orange juice

Bring a saucepan of water to the boil. Add the asparagus and blanch for 2 minutes. Immediately refresh under cold water and drain.

To make the dressing, place all the ingredients in a heavy-bottomed saucepan. Bring to the boil, reduce the heat and simmer very gently until syrupy. Set aside.

Heat a griddle pan. Baste the asparagus, courgette and red pepper with 2 tablespoons of the olive oil and cook in the griddle pan until charred on all sides. You will have to do this in batches. Transfer to a bowl and add a tablespoon of the dressing. Gently toss the vegetables in the dressing to coat.

Mix the chopped parsley into the butterbeans, together with the tablespoon of reserved butterbean liquid, the remaining tablespoon of olive oil and a dash of Tabasco. Transfer to a plate and top with the warm vegetables. Serve with a little of the dressing drizzled over each plate.

Broad beans with straw mushrooms, baby spinach and goat's cheese

I slip the broad beans from their skins, as you can see from the picture, but don't feel remotely guilty if you don't – in fact, I think there is quite a lot to be said for keeping them on, as long as they're not too thick and tough. I used a delicious Golden Cross chèvre with a layer of ash between the cheese and rind, which is exquisite when cut.

SERVES 4
550 g/1 lb 4 oz frozen broad beans
3 tablespoons olive oil
1 teaspoon tamari
2 teaspoons balsamic vinegar
1 garlic clove, crushed
8 whole artichoke hearts bottled in olive oil, sliced
8 sun-dried tomatoes, cut into smaller slices
60 g/2 oz straw mushrooms, cut in half (optional)
12 small new potatoes, cut into thick slices
sea salt
60 g/2 oz baby spinach, ready washed
150 g/5 oz goat's cheese, crumbly or soft

Bring a saucepan of salted water to the boil. Add the broad beans and bring back to the boil for 5–7 minutes until tender.

Meanwhile, in a bowl, mix together 2 tablespoons of the olive oil, the tamari, balsamic vinegar, garlic, artichokes, sun-dried tomatoes and the straw mushrooms if using.

When they are ready, drain the broad beans and add to the bowl.

Heat a griddle pan and add the remaining 1 tablespoon of olive oil. Fry the slices of potato on both sides until golden brown and tender. Sprinkle with salt and immediately add to the rest of the salad, adding the spinach leaves at the last possible moment and then topping with the cheese. Eat at once.

Baby spinach, seared mango, sesame seeds, fried tofu

I very much wanted to include this salad – the mango, spinach and tofu sit so well together – but because it has with slight variations appeared in all three of my previous books, I felt that I had to come up with yet another twist to it. I stared into the cupboards for an age, then my hand just went to the ginger cordial.

SERVES 2
275 g/10 oz firm tofu, cut into about 12 quite thick slices
1 tablespoon tamari
2 tablespoons olive oil
1 tablespoon sesame seeds
1 smallish mango, ripe, sweet and firm, cut into about 12 slices
250 g/9 oz baby spinach, washed
½ small red onion, sliced paper thin
sea salt and freshly ground black pepper

dressing
1 tablespoon pink ginger cordial or syrup from a jar of preserved ginger
1 tablespoon soft brown sugar
2 cm/1 inch piece of ginger, grated and squeezed, and the resulting liquid reserved
dash of Tabasco sauce

First dip the tofu slices into the tamari and set aside.

Heat 1 tablespoon of the olive oil in a frying pan. Add the tofu and sesame seeds and fry until the tofu is golden brown all over, crisping up in places and amply covered in the seeds. Remove the tofu from the pan, adding any remaining sesame seeds to the tofu.

Heat the rest of the olive oil in the same frying pan. Add the mango and quickly sauté for a few seconds on both sides so that it becomes beautifully seared and caramelized.

Toss the spinach quickly in a hot saucepan until it wilts, then squeeze out any excess liquid. Add the onion, reserving some for garnish. Season lightly with salt and pepper and a dash of olive oil. Keep all the components warm while you make the dressing.

To the same frying pan that you used for the tofu and mango, add the ginger cordial or syrup and sugar and warm over a gentle heat until the sugar is completely dissolved and the liquid just begins to bubble, which will only take a minute or two. Quickly stir in the squeezed ginger juice and Tabasco. Remove from the heat.

To serve, divide the spinach between two plates. Top with the mango slices and the sesame-covered tofu. Pour the dressing over and around and serve.

Pasta with your eyes shut It may seem all too obvious, but pasta is so quick, so versatile, so simple that I cook it at least twice a week. When it comes to pasta we all have our old faithfuls, recipes that never let us down, that we can cook 'with our eyes shut' – and these are some of mine.

Pappardelle with porcini and brandy

Every 250 g packet of pappardelle I have come across says it serves four. This is fine as a starter portion, eaten as the Italians do to precede another main course, but eaten the way most of the rest of us eat pasta, it is not. In fact, I find that it makes exactly three good portions. I like to serve whole roasted tomatoes on the side as well as a dish of wilted spinach and a green salad.

SERVES 3–4
1 tablespoon olive oil
250 g/9 oz pappardelle
25 g/scant 1 oz butter
2–3 garlic cloves, very finely chopped or crushed
1 tablespoon brandy
about 50 g/1½ oz dried sliced porcini mushrooms soaked in 300 ml/10 fl oz hot water
  for 10 minutes
8 tablespoons double cream
1 small bunch of fresh basil
sea salt and freshly ground black pepper
freshly grated Parmesan, to serve (optional)

Bring a large saucepan of salted water to the boil with the olive oil added to it. Cook the pasta according to packet instructions.

Meanwhile, melt the butter in a small saucepan. Add the garlic and stir well with a fork or tiny whisk. Add the brandy, continuing to whisk. Add the mushrooms, but reserve their soaking water, and cook for a minute. Then add the cream and simmer for another minute. Now add the mushroom water and leave to bubble gently for about 10 minutes, by which time it should have reduced by about one third. Add a small sprig of basil in the last couple of minutes, then fish it out before the end. The sauce should be ready at pretty much the same time as the pasta.

Drain the pasta very well, return it to the still hot saucepan and pour the sauce all over it. Mix well and serve at once, garnished with the rest of the basil, picked off the stalks, with or without Parmesan.

Linguine with petits pois, braised Little Gem lettuce, Parmesan and garlic

This takes the classic French dish of petits pois braised with lettuce, deconstructs it and puts the lettuces on top.

SERVES 2
2 tablespoons olive oil
2 shallots, finely chopped
2 garlic cloves, sliced
200 g/7 oz frozen petits pois
100 ml/3½ fl oz double cream
sea salt and freshly ground black pepper
2 Little Gem lettuces, quartered
100 ml/3½ fl oz hot vegetable stock, made with a pinch of bouillon powder
350 g/12 oz fresh linguine
30 g/1 oz Parmesan, grated or shaved

Bring a large saucepan of salted water to the boil.

Heat 1 tablespoon of the olive oil in a frying pan and fry the shallots and 1 garlic clove until translucent. Add the petits pois, stir for 3–4 minutes, and when they are completely thawed out add the cream. Season with salt and pepper, then simmer for 2–3 minutes. Transfer to a large warmed bowl and keep warm.

In the same frying pan, lightly fry the second garlic clove in the remaining olive oil. Add the quartered lettuces and hot stock and braise for 10 minutes or until tender, so that most, if not all, of the liquid has evaporated.

Meanwhile, boil the pasta for about 4 minutes or according to packet instructions. Drain thoroughly and mix into the peas and cream. Place the lettuce and Parmesan on top and serve at once.

Spaghetti
with diced tomatoes, sliced garlic and rocket

Fresh, summery, colourful and quick, this is practically a no-cook sauce.

SERVES 2
250 g/9 oz spaghetti
4 tablespoons olive oil
6 large garlic cloves, finely sliced
900 g/2 lb ripe red tomatoes, deseeded and chopped
12 black olives, stoned
sea salt and freshly ground black pepper
50 g/1½ oz rocket
1 tablespoon pistachios, roughly broken up
freshly grated Parmesan, to serve

Bring a large saucepan of salted water to the boil. Drop in the spaghetti and cook for about 12 minutes or according to packet instructions.

Meanwhile, heat the oil in a frying pan. Add the garlic and fry until just beginning to colour. Take the oil off the heat, remove the garlic and set it aside. Just before the pasta is cooked, return the oil to a very gentle heat to warm through.

Drain the pasta as soon as it is cooked and add the warmed oil, garlic, chopped tomatoes, black olives and salt and pepper to taste, and the rocket so it wilts in the heat. Gently stir in the pistachios, reserving a few pieces for garnish.

Serve at once, topped with the rest of the pistachios and with Parmesan on the side.

Linguine with olive oil, lemon, basil, Parmesan and black pepper

Use fresh pasta and you have an elegant pasta dish in five minutes. Make sure your serving bowl can withstand a gentle oven heat.

SERVES 4
120 ml/4 fl oz extra virgin olive oil
50 g/1½ oz Parmesan, grated
2 garlic cloves, crushed
freshly ground black pepper
juice of 1 lemon, plus zest for garnish
500 g/1 lb 2 oz dried linguine or 750g/1 lb 11 oz if using fresh
handful of fresh basil, roughly chopped, a few leaves reserved for garnish

Bring a large saucepan of salted water to the boil.

Meanwhile, put the olive oil, Parmesan, garlic, black pepper and lemon juice in a bowl large enough to receive the pasta. Put the bowl in a medium hot oven.

Cook the pasta – about 4 minutes if it is fresh, usually 12–14 if it isn't (follow the instructions on the packet) – then drain it thoroughly and immediately mix it with the warmed oil mixture.

Garnish with the reserved basil and lemon zest and serve at once.

Spaghetti
with roasted tomato sauce

Serve with a generous bowl of very good Parmesan and a hot baguette spread with garlic and basil butter – simply delicious.

SERVES 2
500 g/1 lb 2 oz ripe tomatoes, halved
3 tablespoons olive oil
2 garlic cloves, crushed
sea salt and freshly ground black pepper
pinch of sugar (optional)
handful of fresh basil
250 g/9 oz spaghetti

Preheat the oven to 230°C/450°F/gas 8. Baste the tomato halves with the olive oil, garlic and salt and pepper – and a pinch of sugar if you want to bring out the ripe, sweet flavour – and roast for 20 minutes. Blend the tomatoes to a purée while still hot, then stir in the fresh basil.

Meanwhile, bring a large saucepan of salted water to the boil. Cook the spaghetti according to packet instructions. Drain the pasta and toss with the sauce. Serve at once.

Ring the changes with one of the following:
cubes of mozzarella added to the hot sauce
50 g/1½ oz black olives
griddled or fried chunks of aubergine
a can of drained cannellini beans
a handful of wilted spinach or rocket

Another suggestion is to cut a head of fennel into four lengths and braise gently in a little water, with sliced garlic and olive oil, then add to the sauce when tender.

Spaghetti with pesto

See page 15 for the basil pesto recipe. Or use a good-quality bought one: Italian delis sometimes have a big tub of their home-made pesto. Mixing my starches – in this case pasta and potato – is not something I would normally go for but I am surprised at how well this works, the pesto clinging differently to the one than to the other.

SERVES 2
250 g/9 oz spaghetti
4–6 small new potatoes, scrubbed and sliced a little less than ½ cm/¼ inch thick
100 g/3½ oz green beans, topped and tailed
70 g/generous 2 oz basil pesto
sea salt and freshly ground black pepper
30 g/1 oz Parmesan, grated or shaved

Bring a large saucepan of salted water to the boil. Add the spaghetti and cook according to packet instructions. Halfway through cooking, add the potatoes and green beans.

While they finish cooking, put the pesto in a large serving bowl with a tablespoon of the hot cooking water.

When the pasta is cooked, drain and add to the pesto. Toss well but delicately so the potatoes don't break up. Season with salt to taste.

Serve immediately with freshly ground black pepper and Parmesan, either on top or on the side.

Spaghetti with radicchio, Fontina cheese and walnuts

The bitterness of radicchio is not to everyone's liking, but you will find that the wine and the balancing strength of the Fontina cheese make for a dish that is not so much bitter as bittersweet – a sophisticated experience indeed. With trevise, the elongated version of radicchio, the bitterness will be further subdued.

SERVES 2
4 tablespoons olive oil or 2 tablespoons olive oil and 30 g/1 oz butter
1 red onion, finely chopped
1 garlic clove, sliced
400 g/14 oz radicchio, about 2 large heads, shredded
5 tablespoons white wine
100 ml/3½ fl oz vegetable stock, made with a pinch of bouillon powder
100 g/3½ oz Fontina cheese, cut into small cubes
handful of fresh basil
handful of fresh parsley, finely chopped
250 g/9 oz fresh spaghetti
sea salt and freshly ground black pepper
2 walnuts, shelled and roughly broken up
60 g/2 oz Parmesan, shaved (optional)

Bring a large saucepan of salted water to the boil. Add 1 tablespoon of the olive oil and then let it simmer until you need it.

Meanwhile, heat half the remaining olive oil, and the butter if using, in a frying pan. Add the onion and fry until soft and just beginning to brown. Add the garlic and fry for a further minute or two. Then add the radicchio and fry until the red turns to brown, which will take a couple of minutes. Add the white wine and stock, bring to the boil and allow to simmer until the liquid is reduced. Then add the Fontina cheese and most of the herbs and just let it sit there for a moment.

Bring the saucepan of water back to the boil. Drop in the spaghetti and cook for about 2–3 minutes. Drain immediately and stir into the hot radicchio mixture. The cheese will melt in the heat. Season with salt and pepper to taste.

Serve immediately, garnished with the remaining herbs, walnut pieces and Parmesan shavings if using.

Spaghetti with nearly scrambled eggs, crispy fried onions and deep-fried sage

This works much better with dried rather than fresh pasta. Because you need to stir the pasta to thicken the egg, I find that fresh begins to go a little pasty. Dried gives you time while the pasta is cooking to fry the onion and sage leaves and to have a very sumptuous pasta dish in 15 minutes.

SERVES 2
300 g/11 oz spaghetti
4 large free range eggs
4 tablespoons double cream
sea salt and freshly ground black pepper
6 tablespoons light olive oil
half a large onion, sliced into thin half moons
small handful of sage leaves
1 lemon, cut into wedges

Bring a large saucepan of salted water to the boil. Add the pasta and cook according to packet instructions.

Meanwhile, beat the eggs with the cream and season with salt and pepper to taste. Place two serving bowls in a medium hot oven.

Heat the olive oil in a small frying pan. Add the onion and fry until golden brown and crispy. Remove with a slotted spoon and drain on kitchen paper; keep the oil hot.

When the pasta is cooked, drain it and return it to its still hot saucepan. Immediately pour on the egg mixture and stir gently on a very low heat until the egg and cream thickens. Remove it from the heat, giving it one last large-stroked stir while you quickly (a matter of seconds) fry the sage leaves in the pan you fried the onion in.

Immediately transfer the pasta to the warmed bowls and top with the crispy fried onion and sage leaves. Serve the lemon wedges on the side. A green salad with an astringent dressing and maybe some cornichons goes well with this.

Orecchiette with broccoli, almonds and Taleggio

SERVES 2
250 g/9 oz orecchiette
4 tablespoons olive oil
2 garlic cloves, finely chopped
2 medium leeks, trimmed and sliced
sea salt and freshly ground black pepper
450 g/1 lb broccoli, cut into florets
100 ml/3½ fl oz white wine
50 g/1½ oz Taleggio, or other soft cheese such as Brie, cut into small cubes
50 g/1½ oz almonds, roasted and chopped into slivers

Bring a large saucepan of salted water to the boil. Cook the orecchiette for 12–14 minutes or according to packet instructions.

Meanwhile, heat the olive oil in a frying pan. Add the garlic and leeks and sauté for 2–3 minutes until translucent. Season with a little salt and pepper to taste and add the broccoli florets. Continue to sauté for a minute, then add about half the wine. Cook until it has all evaporated, then add the rest of the wine and simmer over a medium heat until it is well reduced – about another 3–4 minutes.

Drain the pasta and add to the hot vegetable mixture. Stir in the cubes of cheese and the slivered almonds. Serve at once with freshly ground black pepper.

Linguine with asparagus and truffle oil

I refer to this at home as millionaire's pasta (go the whole hog and use a white truffle). You could easily make three family meals for the same cost but if there are just two of you, why not? It's still going to cost less than a mediocre takeaway and the flavours are so delicate, so refined, they imperceptibly instil a kind of peace and munificence. Don't be alarmed by the quantity of truffle oil used. For one thing it has a fleeting taste and for another, the kind I use is primarily olive oil anyway, richly infused with the exotic fungus.

SERVES 2
1 vanilla pod
350 g/12 oz fresh linguine
1 big bundle of asparagus, about 450 g/1 lb, tough ends removed
100 ml/3½ fl oz truffle oil
2 (at least) black truffles, sliced very finely with a vegetable peeler
15 g/½ oz best Parmesan, shaved
freshly ground black pepper

Bring a large saucepan of salted water to the boil. Add the vanilla pod for a minute, then remove with a slotted spoon.

Add the linguine, stir once to loosen, then add the asparagus spears. After 4 minutes, drain thoroughly, transfer to a warmed bowl and immediately pour in the truffle oil.

Divide between two warmed plates and top with the truffles and Parmesan shavings as well as the finest sprinkling of black pepper.

Wonderful eggs and cheese It has become easier to buy free range eggs and even large organic eggs, and, though at a price, they taste as eggs should. Eat fewer of them if necessary but eat only the best. I am quite laissez-faire about most things but about eggs I am fanatic.

Frittata with potatoes, tomatoes and mushrooms

This is a classic standby and I cannot imagine being without these three basic ingredients in my kitchen. An alternative would be with broccoli and Brie. Substitute 200 g/7 oz broccoli florets for the mushrooms, potatoes and tomatoes, and add 150 g/5 oz Brie, ripe and creamy, to the semi-cooked frittata. Another delicious way is with red peppers, feta cheese and black olives, or a mass of wilted spinach and goat's cheese. The possibilities are endless. Just don't overcook.

SERVES 2–4
4 large free range eggs, beaten
2 tablespoons double cream
sea salt and freshly ground black pepper
3 tablespoons olive oil
350 g/12 oz potatoes, peeled and chopped into small cubes
1 garlic clove, sliced
90 g/3 oz (about 8 or 9 mushrooms), whole or halved, depending on size
180 g/6 oz tomatoes, quartered

Whisk the eggs, cream, salt and pepper together and set aside.

Heat 2 tablespoons of the oil in a heavy-bottomed frying pan, add the potatoes and garlic and fry for about 10 minutes, until the potatoes are golden. Add a little water if necessary to prevent the potatoes from sticking to the pan, but always let it evaporate completely and let the pan dry out before adding any more. The potatoes are best when they have crisped up a bit.

Add another spoonful of olive oil to the potatoes and let it heat up. Add the mushrooms and continue to cook for another minute.

Add the quartered tomatoes, season with salt and pepper, and cook for another minute.

Add the egg mixture. Reduce the heat and cook gently until it sets. You will need to cut through it several times to allow the uncooked eggs to run into the gaps and cook too. The easiest way to finish off the top is to flash it under a hot grill for a few carefully watched seconds, until it is just set though still appetizingly soft. Serving a small bowl of chermoula (page 17) by the side or adding a spoonful to the potatoes and mushrooms completely transforms this.

Eggs en cocotte with spinach and cream

I am going to give you a cooking time for this but not to the last minute and only with an imploration to check and check again. In my oven, this took 22 minutes at 190°C but I've seen recipes at 180°C for 20 minutes and 200°C for 18. You know how the egg whites can go from slimy and horrible to perfectly set in a minute and the egg yolks from soft to hard in the time it takes you to untie your apron? In an ideal world, I would love to be able to use half sorrel and half spinach, but how many of us are able to find sorrel? When eggs are the raison d'être, as here, is there any point in using any but the very best?

SERVES 2
4 teaspoons butter, softened
1 tablespoon olive oil
1 garlic clove, very finely chopped (optional)
350 g/12 oz spinach
sea salt and freshly ground black pepper
pinch of freshly grated nutmeg
6 tablespoons double cream
4 large organic free range eggs

Preheat the oven to 190°C/375°F/gas 5. Butter a round 20 cm/8 inch earthenware or other ovenproof dish (or two smaller ones).

Heat the oil in a saucepan, add the garlic, if using, and fry gently until softened. Add the spinach and toss quickly until it wilts slightly. Drain off any excess liquid and season with salt, pepper and nutmeg. Put the spinach mixture in the buttered dish or dishes and make wells in it to receive first the cream and then the carefully cracked eggs.

Bake in the oven for 22 minutes, but see above. Eat at once. (Dare you try an incy wincy bit of harissa with this?)

 'In my teenage, calorie counting years I made these "soufflés" in the search for

Cottage cheese soufflés with thyme

In my teenage, calorie counting years I made these 'soufflés' in the search for something delicious and non-fattening and if you really want to know, no, never with double cream. I am no longer quite so neurotic (and neither thinner nor fatter) so in goes the cream. You can add sautéed sweetcorn kernels to this or some petits pois or a small head of broccoli, broken into florets and blanched in boiling water. Or you can make them very plain and serve these things on the side.

SERVES 4
2 teaspoons butter, melted
2 eggs, separated
50 g/1½ oz Parmesan, grated
100 g/3½ oz cottage cheese
½ teaspoon fresh thyme leaves, chopped
3 tablespoons double cream
sea salt and freshly ground black pepper

Preheat the oven to 180°C/350°F/gas 4. Butter four ramekins with the melted butter.

Mix together the egg yolks, Parmesan, cottage cheese, thyme and cream. Season with salt and pepper and set aside.

Whisk the egg whites until they form soft peaks, then gently fold them into the egg yolk mixture. Pour into the ramekins and bake for 12–15 minutes, until well risen and golden.

Serve at once. A peppery leaf, either rocket or watercress, goes very well with this.

something delicious and non-fattening'

Dolcelatte gnocchi
with broccoli and roasted butternut squash

Despite the long recipe, I promise these are very easy to make and, unlike most gnocchi, pretty strongly flavoured. I don't usually bother to roll them out into thin sausages but just break off pieces the size of large kalamata olives.

SERVES 4

gnocchi
450 g/1 lb ricotta
100 g/3½ oz farina 00 or plain flour
3 tablespoons polenta
3 large egg yolks
good pinch of freshly grated nutmeg
4 tablespoons flat-leaf parsley, chopped
1 large garlic clove, crushed
8 tablespoons (60 g/2 oz in total) walnuts, finely chopped, plus 2 whole walnuts to garnish
90 g/3 oz dolcelatte
freshly ground black pepper

sauce
150 g/5 oz broccoli, florets only
30 g/1 oz butter
100 g/3½ oz dolcelatte
3 tablespoons double cream

roasted butternut squash
1 small butternut squash, seeds removed, but skin left on, cut into 12 long slices
1 tablespoon olive oil
½ teaspoon tamari
dash of Tabasco sauce
sea salt and freshly ground black pepper

Preheat the oven to its highest setting. Baste the butternut squash with olive oil, tamari and Tabasco and season with a little salt and pepper. Place on a baking sheet and roast in the oven until tender and browned, about 25 minutes.

Meanwhile, in a bowl, mix together the gnocchi ingredients and form into a ball with your hands – I tend not to add salt because the dolcelatte is already salty. The mixture should feel sticky and soft. If it comes away from the sides of the bowl too cleanly add a little extra egg yolk or a little more ricotta. Put the mixture in the fridge for a few minutes to rest.

Bring a large saucepan of salted water to the boil. Blanch the broccoli florets for 1 minute and remove with a slotted spoon. Reserve the water to cook the gnocchi, letting it simmer until you are ready.

To make the sauce, place the butter, dolcelatte, cream, 5 tablespoons of the broccoli cooking water and some black pepper in a small saucepan over a gentle heat. Allow to melt, stirring a couple of times. Set aside.

Using your lightly floured hands, shape the gnocchi into 4 cm/2 inch pieces. They can be quite roughly shaped or you can make long thin sausages and cut them into smaller lengths. Keep flouring your hands to stop them from sticking to the mixture.

Bring the saucepan of water back to the boil. Test that the gnocchi is firm enough by dropping one into the boiling water. If it rises to the surface without collapsing (this should take about 45 seconds), it is fine, if not, it simply needs a little more flour. Drop the gnocchi into the water in batches, giving them about 40 seconds or so after they have risen to cook. Remove with a slotted spoon to a warmed plate.

Reheat the sauce, add the broccoli and warm through. Divide the sauce between four warmed plates, place the gnocchi on top, season with black pepper and add 2 or 3 slices of butternut squash. Serve any remaining squash separately.

Feta cheese soufflés with black olive toasts

These will, of course, deflate as they cool. Though no less delicious and creamy for it, it would be such a shame not to revel in their golden and risen perfection, so make sure everything else is just so and your people are sitting at the table ready and waiting.

SERVES 4
30 g/1 oz butter, plus extra for buttering the ramekins
30 g/1 oz plain flour
150 ml/5 fl oz milk
2 egg yolks
1 tablespoon freshly grated Parmesan, plus extra for sprinkling
125 g/4 oz feta cheese, chopped
pinch of freshly grated nutmeg
1½ egg whites

to serve
2 tablespoons light and fruity olive oil
1 red pepper, deseeded and cut into 8 strips
4 slices of toast, cut into triangles
about 50 g/1½ oz black olives, roughly chopped
1 bunch of watercress
vinaigrette (page 16)

Preheat the oven to 180°C/350°F/gas 4. Butter four ramekins.

To make the soufflés, melt the butter in a small saucepan. Stir in the flour and cook over a medium heat for 1 minute. Remove from the heat and gradually whisk in the milk. Return to a low heat, whisking constantly until the sauce boils and thickens. Remove from the heat again and whisk in the egg yolks, cheeses and nutmeg.

Whisk the egg whites until they form soft peaks, then gently fold them into the warm sauce. Spoon into the ramekins and bake in a bain-marie in the oven for 20 minutes or until well risen and brown. Switch off the oven but leave them in there for a further minute with the door open.

Meanwhile, heat a griddle pan. Use 1 tablespoon of the olive oil to baste the red pepper, then griddle until softened. Transfer to a plate and drizzle over another tablespoon of olive oil. Arrange on the toast triangles, then top with the black olives. Dress the watercress lightly with vinaigrette and serve alongside the soufflés.

Swiss cheese fondue

Fondue is strictly cold weather fare and the Swiss have got the eating of it down to a scientific fine art. Drink either wine – more of whatever you have put into the fondue, so choose well – or a warm drink, but never cold water, which congeals the cheese and causes God knows what grief. Eat an astringent salad of onions to cut through all the cholesterol and plenty of carbohydrates – bread and potatoes – for balance.

SERVES 4–6
1 large garlic clove, cut in half
400 ml/14 fl oz dry white wine, such as muscadet
1 teaspoon fresh lemon juice
350 g/12 oz Gruyère, grated
350 g/12 oz Emmental, grated
1 teaspoon cornflour
2 tablespoons kirsch
large pinch of freshly grated nutmeg

onion salad
4 large sweet onions, very finely sliced
4 tablespoons groundnut oil
1 teaspoon wine vinegar
2 teaspoons strong Dijon mustard
1 tablespoon dry white wine, as above
sea salt and freshly ground black pepper

to serve
1 or 2 day old baguette, cut into bite-sized pieces
bowl of new potatoes, freshly boiled
onion salad, as above, or sauerkraut

To make the onion salad, bring a saucepan of salted water to the boil. Add the sliced onions, turn off the heat and soak until soft, about 5 minutes. Drain well. Make a dressing with the remaining salad ingredients and mix with the warm onions. Leave to cool.

Rub the inside of a saucepan or fondue pot with the cut garlic. Pour in the wine and lemon juice and heat over a gentle flame until it reaches simmering point. Turn the heat down low and add both the cheeses, a handful at a time, continuously stirring with a wooden spoon so the cheese just bubbles and slowly melts into the wine to form a smooth sauce.

Mix the cornflour and kirsch in a separate bowl then slowly stir into the fondue until it becomes smooth again. Season to taste with nutmeg and pepper and transfer to a fondue burner at the table. Serve with the bread, potatoes and onion salad or sauerkraut and a green salad if you wish.

7

Sexy tarts and easy pies

Ready-made (and sometimes ready-rolled) puff pastry is getting better and better, making it perfectly plausible to get a homely pie or a seductive tart, topped to the hilt with vegetables, on to the table in 30 minutes or less.

White onion tart with Parmesan

White onions have an almost unbelievable sweetness to them and so are not as sharp as regular onions, though still unmistakably, tear-jerkingly pure onion. They can be used to make a most wonderful cream of onion soup and in this tart are refined, delicate, elegant – all those sorts of words.

SERVES 2–4
250 g/9 oz puff pastry
3 tablespoons truffle oil or light olive oil
2 white onions, about 700 g/1lb 9 oz, very finely sliced
2 garlic cloves, crushed
sea salt and freshly ground black pepper
1 small egg, beaten, for glazing
30 g/1 oz Parmesan, shaved
1 black truffle, finely shaved (optional)

Preheat the oven to its highest setting. On a lightly floured surface, roll out the pastry to a 30 cm/12 inch circle, using the base of a loose-bottomed tart tin as a template. Lightly flour this base and slide under the pastry circle. Prick all over with a fork, leaving a 2 cm/1 inch rim all the way around. Set aside.

Very gently heat the truffle or olive oil in a frying pan. Add the onions and garlic and sweat over a very low heat so that the onion does not brown in the slightest and maintains a little bite. Pile the onion onto the puff pastry, leaving the unpricked edge clear. Season with salt and pepper, then brush the exposed pastry with the egg.

Place in the hot oven for 20 minutes; some of the onion will be tinged with brown.

Remove from the oven and top with the Parmesan and truffle shavings, if using. Delicious with a watercress salad, lightly dressed with light olive oil and a dash of balsamic vinegar.

Cherry tomato tart
with black olives, red onion and goat's cheese

'Oh, but cherry tomatoes are so vulgar,' someone said to me recently. Well, then vulgar I shall be.

SERVES 2–4
250 g/9 oz puff pastry
3 tablespoons sun-dried tomato purée
750 g/1 lb 11 oz cherry tomatoes
1 tablespoon olive oil
1 small red onion, peeled and cut into wedges
4 garlic cloves, peeled and left whole
30 g/1 oz black olives, stoned
75 g/2½ oz goat's cheese, soft or crumbly
sea salt and freshly ground black pepper
1 small egg, beaten, for glazing
several sprigs of fresh basil, to garnish

Preheat the oven to its highest setting. On a lightly floured surface, roll out the pastry to a 30 cm/12 inch circle, using the base of a loose-bottomed tart tin as a template. Lightly flour this base and slide under the pastry circle. Prick all over with a fork, leaving a 2 cm/1 inch edge. Spread the tomato purée all over, except for the unpricked edge.

Baste the cherry tomatoes with the olive oil and pack as tightly as you can on top of the purée. Sneak in the onion wedges, garlic cloves and the olives, dot the goat's cheese here and there, season with salt and pepper and brush the pastry rim with the egg.

Place in the hot oven for 20–25 minutes, by which time many of the tomatoes will have blistered, browned and burst. Garnish with sprigs of basil and serve with a green salad.

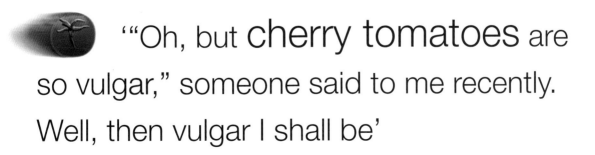

'"Oh, but cherry tomatoes are so vulgar," someone said to me recently. Well, then vulgar I shall be'

Red pepper, courgette, black olive
and Manchego cheese tart

SERVES 2–4
250 g/9 oz puff pastry
1 long thin sweet red pepper, deseeded, pith removed and cut into 8
2 medium courgettes, cut into ½ cm/¼ inch thick slices
3 tablespoons olive oil
dash of balsamic vinegar
1 red onion, very thinly sliced
90 g/3 oz Manchego cheese, cubed
12 black olives, stoned
sea salt and freshly ground black pepper
1 small egg, beaten, for glazing

Preheat the oven to its highest setting. On a lightly floured surface, roll out the pastry to a 30 cm/12 inch circle, using the base of a loose-bottomed tart tin as a template. Lightly flour this base and slide under the pastry circle. Prick all over with a fork, leaving a 2 cm/1 inch rim all the way around and set aside.

Heat a griddle pan or frying pan. Place the red pepper and courgettes in the pan, pour over 2 tablespoons of the oil and griddle until blackened in places, about 5–7 minutes. Stir in the balsamic vinegar.

Spread the onion over the pastry, leaving the unpricked edge clear, and place the griddled vegetables on top. Tuck the cheese and olives in between the vegetables, season with salt and pepper and drizzle with the remaining olive oil. Brush the edge with the beaten egg and bake in the hot oven for 20 minutes.

Mushroom and tarragon tart with brandy and cream

SERVES 2–4
250 g/9 oz puff pastry
2 teaspoons olive oil
450 g/1 lb chestnut mushrooms, brushed clean if necessary
2 teaspoons tamari
2 garlic cloves, crushed
1 tablespoon brandy
sprig of tarragon, finely chopped
dash of Tabasco sauce
5 tablespoons double cream
sea salt and freshly ground black pepper
1 small egg, beaten, for glazing

Preheat the oven to its highest setting.On a lightly floured surface, roll out the pastry to a 30 cm/12 inch circle, using the base of a loose-bottomed tart tin as a template. Lightly flour this base and slide under the pastry circle. Prick all over with a fork, leaving a 2 cm/1 inch rim all the way round. Set aside.

Heat the oil in a frying pan, add the mushrooms and cook until they sizzle and squeak in that disconcerting way that makes you think they might be alive after all. Add the tamari and as it sizzles in the pan add a drop or two of water to revive it. Add the garlic and continue cooking until the mushrooms have no trace of white rawness left – this shouldn't take more than a couple of minutes on a carefully monitored but fierce heat.

Add the brandy and tarragon, Tabasco and cream. Bring to the boil until the brandy is an evocative rather than overpowering presence. Adjust the seasoning and allow to cool for a few minutes.

Place on top of the pastry, leaving the unpricked edge clear. Brush the edge with the egg and bake in the hot oven for 20 minutes. Serve with a green salad and perhaps some Grilled courgettes (page 28, but omit the yoghurt).

Spanakopita

SERVES 4
2 tablespoons olive oil
1 red onion, finely chopped
2 garlic cloves, crushed
450 g/1 lb baby spinach, ready washed
30 g/1 oz butter
250 g/9 oz feta cheese, cubed
pinch of freshly grated nutmeg
sea salt and freshly ground black pepper
filo pastry, 10 sheets, 30 x 12 cm/12 x 7 inches
1 teaspoon sesame seeds

Preheat the oven to its highest setting.

Heat the oil in a large, heavy-bottomed saucepan. Add the onion and garlic and fry until translucent. Add the spinach and cook until it wilts, turning it over a couple of times.

Place the butter in a small ovenproof dish and put in the oven to melt for a minute.

Add the feta cheese to the spinach and onion mixture and season to taste with nutmeg, salt and pepper.

Brush the bottom of a 23 cm/9 inch loose-bottomed tart tin with a little of the melted butter. Line with a sheet of filo pastry, brush with butter and lay another sheet of filo on top at a 90° angle to the first, so that you make a cross, and brush with butter. Repeat until you have used up five sheets. Add the spinach filling. Fold the excess pastry from the bottom over it and cover with the five remaining sheets, again criss-crossing and brushing with butter between each layer, folding the excess pastry under each time. Finish with a brushing of melted butter and a sprinkling of sesame seeds. Remove the outer ring of the tart tin and bake the pie in the hot oven for 15 minutes.

For a more even bake, halfway through you can invert the pie on to a plate, then slide it back on to the base and into the oven, so that it browns properly on both sides.

Serve with a quickly thrown together Greek salad and a bowl of kalamata olives.

Saffron potato, spinach and Fontina cheese pie

You can use a floury or a waxy potato for this. Of course, the result will be different – more homely with the former, smarter and more held together with the latter. I use organic chestnut mushrooms, but you could add porcini mushrooms, reconstituted in the way so often described in this book, or even button mushrooms – just as long as you first sauté them until the juices have wept and then reduced to almost nothing, thus intensifying the texture and taste. Ready-washed spinach is easy, or you could use frozen if you have the forethought to remove it from the freezer before leaving for work in the morning. I am not that organised.

SERVES 4–6
350 g/12 oz puff pastry
500 g/1 lb 2 oz new potatoes, with skins left on, sliced no more than ½ cm/¼ inch thick
3 tablespoons olive oil
3 garlic cloves, finely sliced
good pinch of best quality saffron strands
sea salt and freshly ground black pepper
200 g/7 oz chestnut mushrooms, sliced
½ teaspoon tamari
dash of Tabasco sauce
200 g/7 oz baby spinach, washed
good pinch of freshly grated nutmeg
150 g/5 oz Fontina cheese, finely sliced
1 large free range egg, beaten, for glazing

Preheat the oven to its highest setting. Take the puff pastry out of the fridge to come to room temperature while you prepare the rest of the ingredients.

In a large saucepan (I like to use my pressure cooker), pour in 300 ml/10 fl oz water, then add the potatoes, all but a teaspoon or so of the olive oil, the garlic, saffron, salt and pepper. Bring to the boil and continue boiling until about half the water is reduced, the rest combining with the olive oil, saffron and garlic to begin to yield a syrupy sauce. When the potatoes are beginning to soften, reduce the heat and continue to simmer gently for about 5 minutes or until the potatoes are tender, glazed in the saffrony sauce and there is no excess watery liquid in the pan.

Meanwhile, heat the rest of the oil in a frying pan. Add the mushrooms and sauté, adding the tamari and Tabasco when the mushrooms are no longer raw. Should they begin to stick, add a little of the liquid from the potatoes. The tamari must not burn, so continue to loosen with potato water as necessary.

While the potatoes are cooking you may have time to toss the spinach in a hot pan until it wilts. Then season it with salt, pepper and nutmeg (though you could wait to do this until

the potatoes are removed from their pan, then wilt the spinach in the same pan to mop up any sticky, delicious sauce that remains there).

Roll out the pastry large enough to fit your dish – round, square or oblong, glass or earthenware, it hardly matters: this is a bottomless pie and the pastry top will cook just as well in any vessel. Set the pastry aside while you fill the dish.

Taste and adjust the seasoning of all components and then layer them in the dish as follows: first the potatoes, then the spinach, then the cheese, finally the mushrooms. Since you will not need the whole of the egg for glazing, you can pour about half of it into the pie; it will only benefit. Now cover with the puff pastry , tucking it in around the edges. Glaze with the rest of the egg and make small holes in the pastry at regular intervals with the point of a small knife.

Bake in the hot oven for 15–20 minutes, until the top is a deep golden brown.

Some baby vegetables and vinaigrette or a mound of watercress and a plate of sliced tomatoes lightly dressed is all you'll need to go with this, but I've also served it with Grilled courgettes with lemon and yoghurt (page 28) and with glazed baby carrots.

Courgettes and patty-pan squash tart
with pine nuts and raisins

I was a late convert to the griddle pan, but now that I do have one, I can hardly leave it alone. It's pretty useful in this recipe because, if you want the tart cooked in the minimum of time, the patty-pans especially need to be helped on their way. The raisins or sultanas need to be as plump as possible. I use Australian ones, which look exactly like what they are – fat dried grapes. Italian pine nuts are leaner, longer and tastier than others, but of course the more common ones will do. Alternatively, substitute with slivered almonds.

SERVES 2–4
1 dessertspoon Dijon mustard
1 garlic clove, crushed
1 tablespoon balsamic vinegar
1 tablespoon tamari
sea salt and freshly ground black pepper
4 tablespoons olive oil, plus a little extra
2 large or 4 small courgettes, cut into ½ cm/¼ inch thick slices
1 large or 2 small red onions, cut into 4 or 6 wedges, depending on size
200 g/7 oz patty-pan squash, yellow and green, cut in half through the top
250 g/9 oz puff pastry
1 small egg, beaten, for glazing
2 tablespoons raisins or sultanas, soaked in wine, muscatel if possible
1 tablespoon (generous) pine nuts

Preheat the oven to its highest setting.

Mix together the mustard, garlic, balsamic vinegar, tamari, a good pinch of salt and 4 tablespoons of olive oil, then mix in the courgettes, red onions and patty-pans.

Heat the griddle pan, wipe with oil and griddle the marinated vegetables in batches so that they are striped with brown in that picturesque barbecued way and their rawness is softened in the searing heat. This should only take about 5 minutes. Hold back some of the marinade.

On a lightly floured surface, roll out the puff pastry to a 30 cm/12 inch circle, using the base of a loose-bottomed tart tin as a template. Lightly flour this base, then slide under the pastry. Prick all over with a fork, leaving a 2 cm/1 inch gap all the way around. Pile the vegetables on top, leaving the unpricked edge clear. Baste the vegetables with most of the remaining marinade and brush the edge of the pastry with the beaten egg.

Bake in the hot oven for 20 minutes. Five minutes before the end of the cooking time scatter over the raisins or sultanas and pine nuts. Drizzle or brush any remaining marinade on top before serving.

Green tart

This is based on a recipe by Claudia Roden but by necessity is made with puff pastry (for speed). It works surprisingly well, with the sides rising up all around the filling. I've also added 3 tablespoons of double cream, a little lemon juice and nutmeg to the spinach, which changes its character somewhat, and the artichokes I use are bottled in oil, rather than canned.

SERVES 4–6
350 g/12 oz puff pastry
3 tablespoons extra virgin olive oil
1 medium onion, diced
2 garlic cloves, finely sliced
250 g/9 oz Italian roasted artichoke hearts in olive oil, cut in half
500 g/1 lb 2 oz frozen petits pois
250 g/9 oz spinach
pinch of freshly grated nutmeg
sea salt and freshly ground black pepper
2 eggs, beaten
freshly squeezed lemon juice
3 tablespoons double cream

Preheat the oven to its highest setting. On a lightly floured surface, roll out the pastry to a 30 cm/12 inch circle, using the base of a loose-bottomed tart tin as a template. Lightly flour this base and slide under the puff pastry circle. Prick all over with a fork, leaving a 2 cm/1 inch gap all the way around, and set aside.

Heat the oil in a frying pan. Add the onion and sauté until soft and golden. Add the garlic and stir. Then add the artichokes, petits pois, spinach and nutmeg. Press the spinach down, cover with a lid and cook. The spinach will wilt, releasing some of its liquid, which will help the petits pois to cook. When the spinach is completely wilted, remove the lid. Continue to cook for another 6 minutes, when the liquid will have all but dried out. Season to taste with salt and pepper.

Remove the spinach mixture from the heat and stir in the eggs, lemon juice to taste and cream. Pour the mixture over the pastry base, leaving the unpricked edge clear. Because this is being cooked at such a high heat, loosely cover the filling with a piece of foil or baking parchment. Bake for 20 minutes, until the egg is cooked but still quite soft and the pastry is cooked through. If you like, you can pour over a little more cream just before serving.

Tarte fine

An Israeli cousin gave me a very simple pastry recipe using cups – two of flour to one of wine – that I have measured out. Since then I have eaten a tarte Alsacienne, made with a pastry no one would give me the recipe for but which is a dead ringer for this one. The only thing is you must roll it out paper thin or it won't taste very nice. Also (don't shoot!), I think this takes about 32 minutes from start to finish. You could, of course, continue in the same vein as the rest of the tarts in this book and use a very thinly rolled out puff pastry sheet instead. An alternative filling would be to spread the pastry with crème fraîche, then goat's cheese – Golden Cross if possible – then drizzle with maple syrup.

SERVES 2–4
225 g/8 oz plain flour, plus more for your hands
100 ml/3½ fl oz white wine
½ teaspoon salt and a pinch of black pepper

filling
1 teaspoon butter
1 large chicory, about 200 g/7 oz, very finely sliced
1 teaspoon soft brown sugar
1 tablespoon white wine
8 tablespoons crème fraîche
60 g/2 oz Gruyère, grated
freshly ground black pepper

Preheat the oven to its highest setting.

To make the pastry, mix all the ingredients together with your hands to form a soft, stretchy dough. Don't be alarmed if at first it looks as if there can't possibly be enough liquid – just persevere and you'll see that there is. Set aside while you make the filling.

Melt the butter in a saucepan and add the chicory; stir to coat the chicory in the butter. Then add the sugar and wine. Cook on a low heat for about 8 minutes. The chicory should be soft and just beginning to colour. Remove from the heat and return to your pastry.

On a lightly floured work surface, roll out the pastry paper thin. Lightly flour a 38 x 35 cm/ 15 x 14 inch baking sheet and place the pastry on top.

Add the crème fraîche and Gruyère to the chicory and spread over the pastry. Bake for about 15 minutes, until the pastry is crisp and golden and the filling bubbling very gently.

Sprinkle a little freshly ground black pepper on top and serve at once with a green salad, more chicory if you are fond of it, some lightly dressed beetroot or some sauerkraut – at any rate, something sharp and vinegary to go with the rich creamy filling.

Bstilla with glazed shallots, prunes and almonds

I never tire of this confit and am constantly finding excuses to make it. Sometimes it goes with great trayfuls of roasted vegetables, other times with a mushroom Wellington, the recipe for which can only go in a book on slow food. (In fact, it is in my first book, *Secrets From A Vegetarian Kitchen*.) It is very rich, and although it is unmistakably savoury, it is also very sweet. Just some simple, blanched broccoli sets it off beautifully.

SERVES 2–4
250 g/9 oz puff pastry, rolled out to 2 rectangles, each 25 x 15 cm/10 x 6 inches
1 small egg, beaten
50 g/1½ oz whole almonds, blanched and skins slipped off
500 g/1 lb 2 oz shallots or small onions
3 tablespoons olive oil
400 g/14 oz soft, ready-to-eat stoned prunes
4 whole garlic cloves, peeled and left whole
2 teaspoons brown sugar
small sprig of parsley or coriander, very finely chopped (optional)
sea salt and freshly ground black pepper
dusting of icing sugar (optional)
pinch of cinnamon

Preheat the oven to its highest setting. Bring a saucepan of water to the boil.

Lightly flour a baking sheet. Make sure the pastry is very thin, about 2 mm/⅒ inch thick. Place the two rectangles side by side on the baking sheet and prick all over with a fork. Then brush lightly with the egg. (Although it is puff pastry, you don't actually want it to rise too much.) Bake the pastry for 15 minutes. If you think you won't forget them in the activity, place the almonds in the oven for 4 minutes to toast lightly.

Meanwhile, blanch the shallots or onions in boiling water for 1 minute, then drain, peel and slice in half.

Heat the olive oil in a saucepan. Measure out 1.25 litres/2 pints of water. Add the shallots or onions to the saucepan and fry until lightly browned. Add the prunes, garlic cloves, sugar and a little of the water. Simmer for 10 minutes on a fierce heat, adding the water gradually. Let it reduce until it starts to caramelise before you add the next lot, so that the shallots are softened and the whole thing is lightly caramelised. When you have used up about three quarters of the water, add the almonds. Finally add your chosen herb and season with salt and pepper.

Now carefully remove the pastry sheets from the oven. Transfer one onto a serving plate. Gently pile the onion, prune and almond confit on top and cover with the second sheet. Dust very lightly with icing sugar, if using, and cinnamon. Serve with broccoli.

Cheats' casseroles and other great ways with vegetables The truth is, most of the recipes in this section, whatever their origin, are really stews, with all the nourishing, warming, convivial attributes the word evokes. They don't take great skill, but you can pack them with flavour.

Chickpea casserole with spinach and red peppers

This is the kind of casserole I used to expect to take hours over and once in a blue moon still do, but it is such a favourite in my family that more often than not I take the shortcut – that is, I use canned chickpeas. Some are very good, very plump, some less so. Ethnic grocery stores often have a large selection and you'll usually find someone to recommend the best to you. The seasoning in this version is more Asian than Moorish but you could, of course, substitute cumin and saffron for coriander and mustard seeds.

SERVES 2
3 tablespoons olive oil
1 small red onion, roughly chopped
1 garlic clove, finely sliced
½ teaspoon ground coriander
½ teaspoon black mustard seeds
400 g/14 oz can chickpeas, including liquid
1 small potato, cut into small chunks
sea salt and freshly ground black pepper
1 red pepper, deseeded, pith removed and cut into 8 strips
125 g/4 oz baby spinach, washed
1 tomato, quartered
2 teaspoons tamari
1 small red chilli, finely chopped

Heat 2 tablespoons of the olive oil in a large saucepan over a medium heat. Add the red onion and garlic and sweat until translucent. Add the ground coriander and the mustard seeds and fry for a minute or so, adding one or two tablespoons of liquid from the can of chickpeas to prevent sticking to the bottom of the pan. Add the chopped potato and stir until well coated with the spices. Season with a little salt and pepper and allow to cook for 5–6 minutes until the potato is almost soft. Then add the chickpeas and the rest of their liquid and simmer gently for 5–7 minutes, until the sauce is thick and rich.

Meanwhile, heat the remaining oil in a griddle pan and sauté the red pepper until charred in places. Add to the chickpeas, then gently add the baby spinach and stir until wilted. Add the tomato and cook until just soft. Finish with the tamari, the chilli and the remaining olive oil, if you like, and some more salt and pepper if necessary.

Serve with a bowl of Greek yoghurt and some lemon wedges as well as some fried or plain tortillas or warmed chapatis.

Mushroom and tofu stroganoff

When I first became a vegetarian, more than 20 years ago, my need for strong flavour led me again and again to mushroom-rich dishes. The mushrooms in cream and brandy, the mushroom tart, the baked whole mushrooms, this stroganoff (hooray for cliché) all hail from those days, but they are recipes that evolve over time and are still some of my favourites. I think the day, very early on, that I discovered what adding a dash of tamari does to the classic marriage of cream, alcohol, onion, mushroom, garlic and a sweet herb such as tarragon, my career path, if I could ever call it that, was set.

SERVES 2–4
200 ml/7 fl oz red wine
2 tablespoons tamari
275 g/10 oz firm plain tofu, cut into 2 cm/1 inch cubes
3 tablespoons groundnut oil
1 medium onion, roughly chopped
5 garlic cloves, chopped
200 g/7 oz chestnut mushrooms, left whole or cut in half
120 ml/4 fl oz double cream
sprig of tarragon
sea salt and freshly ground black pepper

Combine the red wine, tamari and 3 tablespoons of water in a dish. Add the tofu to marinate. Set aside.

Heat 1 tablespoon of the oil in a heavy-bottomed saucepan or frying pan. Add the onion and garlic and fry over a gentle heat until pale golden. Add the mushrooms and continue to sauté for 4–5 minutes until they are cooked through.

In a separate pan, heat the remaining oil and sauté the tofu, adding a little of the marinade at a time until it is slightly less than half used up. The tofu must brown on all sides so keep turning it gently, taking care not to break it up. Then remove from the heat.

Add the cream and half the tarragon sprig to the mushrooms, bring to the boil, reduce the heat and simmer gently for a minute or so. Add the remaining marinade to the mushrooms and simmer for another couple of minutes, until the sauce is creamy and intensely flavoured. Finally, add the fried tofu and the remaining tarragon. Season with salt and pepper and serve with basmati rice.

Sweet potato and shiitake mushrooms
with marmalade and star anise

I made this one February night, when I had just stopped working full time. Partly to keep myself sane and partly because it fulfilled some archetypal fantasy, I had earlier that day made the hugest pot of marmalade. Jars of it lay cooling on my windowsill, amber coloured and glistening, calling out to be used. I started with this casserole, and it has gone into marmalade muffins, a chocolate and marmalade cake, warm marmalade and Cointreau pancakes on Shrove Tuesday and, of course, innumerable pieces of toast.

SERVES 2 GENEROUSLY
½ teaspoon bouillon powder
4 tablespoons olive oil
1 large sweet potato, peeled and cubed
½ butternut squash, peeled and cubed
1 large carrot, peeled and thickly sliced on the slant
2 whole star anise
2–3 teaspoons tamari
dash of Tabasco sauce
200 g/7 oz shiitake mushrooms, cut in half
100 g/3½ oz green beans, topped and tailed
2 cm/1 inch piece of ginger, grated and squeezed, and the resulting liquid reserved
2 tablespoons marmalade
1 tablespoon tamarind paste
juice of half a lime
3 spring onions, chopped on the slant
1 small bunch of coriander, roughly chopped
sea salt and freshly ground black pepper

Bring a small saucepan of water with the bouillon dissolved in it to the boil. You will use this both for blanching the beans and in place of stock.

Heat half the olive oil in a large saucepan. Add the sweet potato, butternut squash, carrot and star anise and sauté for about 5 minutes, until all the vegetables are well coated in the oil and browning lightly. Add a spoonful or two of the hot bouillon water to prevent sticking. Continue to sauté until the sweet potato and butternut squash begin to soften. Add a dash of tamari and Tabasco and, immediately, a little more of the bouillon water and oil. Stir on a fairly high heat for a couple of minutes. Add the shiitake mushrooms and continue to cook.

Now drop the green beans into the boiling bouillon water and blanch for about 5 minutes, continuing to take out spoonfuls of the boiling water to add to the vegetables as you need to. When the green beans are just tender, scoop out using a slotted spoon, reserve

their cooking water, and add them to the rest of the simmering vegetables. Continue to cook over a high heat (adjusting it as necessary) and stirring regularly.

In a separate saucepan, warm the rest of the oil, 2 teaspoons of tamari, 6 tablespoons of the hot green bean water, ginger juice, marmalade, tamarind and lime juice so that the marmalade dissolves and the sauce becomes slightly reduced and thickened.

When the vegetables are soft, nicely browned but still holding their shape, add the sauce, spring onions and coriander, and season to taste with salt and pepper.

Serve with basmati rice. As an alternative to plain rice, you could make coconut rice: replace half the water with unsweetened coconut milk and include a gently bruised stalk of lemongrass, which you remove when the rice is cooked. I would also serve some plain yoghurt flavoured with lime and chopped fresh coriander.

Good old-fashioned veggie stew 'n' dumplings

The timing is tight here: have all the ingredients prepared and to hand. If you do away with the dumplings, then serve the stew with a warmed cottage loaf and herb or garlic butter.

SERVES 4
300 g/11 oz parsnips, smallish, cut lengthways into 4
6 tablespoons olive oil
sea salt and freshly ground black pepper
8 shallots, peeled and cut in half
2 garlic cloves, sliced
350 g/12 oz carrots, peeled and cut into ½ cm/¼ inch slices
350 g/12 oz turnips, cut into 2½ cm/1¼ inch chunks
150 g/5 oz button mushrooms
1 vegetable stock cube, dissolved in 350 ml/12 fl oz water
200 ml/7 fl oz cider
1 bay leaf
1½ teaspoons cornflour

dumplings
125 g/4 oz self-raising flour
50 g/1½ oz Cheddar, grated
3 tablespoons chopped fresh parsley
50 g/1½ oz butter

Preheat the oven to its highest setting. Toss the parsnips with 2 tablespoons of olive oil. Season with a little salt and pepper and roast for about 25 minutes, until golden brown. They may be ready a little before the stew, in which case take them out and set aside.

Heat the remaining oil in a large, heavy-bottomed saucepan. Add the shallots and garlic and fry for 2 minutes, stirring occasionally. Add the carrots and turnips and sauté for about 4 minutes, then add the mushrooms and sauté for a further minute.

Meanwhile, make the dumpling mixture. Lightly mix all the ingredients together and season with salt and pepper. Add about a tablespoon of water to bring it together to form a soft dough. Form into about 16 small walnut-sized balls and set aside.

Add the vegetable stock to the vegetables, along with 175 ml/6 fl oz of the cider and the bay leaf, and let the stew bubble steadily for another 5 minutes, stirring occasionally. Now dissolve the cornflour in the remaining cider, add to the stew and boil to thicken. As soon as it has thickened, place the dumplings in gently, so that they are about three-quarters immersed. Cover with a lid and simmer slowly for 15–17 minutes, until the dumplings are risen, the stew looks rich and the vegetables meltingly soft. If you have not already done so, remove the parsnips from the oven and scatter them over the top.

'Baked beans' with vegetarian sausages

This is the kind of *simple comme bonjour* recipe that I am almost embarrassed to include. Still, when I did a quick survey of what people at work commonly ate as a quick snack, guess what came up most often? So here you are, a recipe for baked beans that still comes out of a can but is about a hundred times more delicious. These are cannellini, not haricot and as for the sausages, you'll find the Quorn ones are best. I like it with warmed bread as I like most things, but you could go the whole hog and serve on toast with a poached egg on top.

SERVES 1
400 g/14 oz can cannellini beans
2 tablespoons sun-dried tomato purée
dash of Tabasco sauce
1 tablespoon olive oil
2 good quality vegetarian sausages
sea salt and freshly ground black pepper
pinch of soft brown sugar (optional)

Empty the can of cannellini beans into a saucepan. Add the sun-dried tomato purée and Tabasco and simmer until hot.

Meanwhile, heat the olive oil in a small frying pan. Cut the sausages into thick slices and fry on all sides until browned. Add to the beans. Season with salt and pepper if you need to and add a pinch of soft brown sugar if you are too conditioned to do without. Simmer together for another minute or two and serve.

Ratatouille

My mother never puts tomatoes in her ratatouille and she cooks it far longer than I do, in a version which is somewhat Moroccanized. For her the redness comes from the paprika, not from the tomatoes. I have written other recipes which are truer to that delicious version but have for a long time now been making this ratatouille with both paprika at the beginning and fresh tomatoes at the end. Remember that aubergine begs to be eaten soft and oily and in this dish takes on an almost confit-like consistency.

SERVES 4
100 ml/3½ fl oz olive oil plus 2 tablespoons
500 g/1 lb 2 oz aubergines, cut into 2–3 cm/1–1½ inch chunks
4 garlic cloves, sliced
1 tablespoon paprika
dash of Tabasco sauce
350 g/12 oz courgettes, cut into 2 cm/1 inch chunks
sea salt and freshly ground black pepper
500 g/1 lb 2 oz peppers, half red and one quarter each yellow and green, deseeded, pith
    removed and cut into 4 cm/2 inch chunks
2 tomatoes, quartered
handful of basil, to garnish

Heat the olive oil in a large saucepan. Add the aubergines and garlic and as soon as they begin to soften, the paprika and Tabasco. Stir continuously over a high heat, adding a little water every time it looks as though the vegetables are sticking to the pan.

While the aubergines are still somewhat firm, add the courgettes. Keep stirring, again adding a little water as necessary and seasoning with salt and pepper. Reduce the heat and allow the vegetables to simmer for a few minutes with a lid on, though you must sneak a peek every so often to make sure that it isn't drying out too much. If it is, add a little more water.

When the aubergines have partly dissolved to a rich, oily paprika mess which has become the background sauce, and the courgettes still have some bite, add in the peppers until they too begin to soften slightly. Finally, stir in the quartered tomatoes and cook until soft but still discernible.

Garnish with the basil and serve with a warm cottage loaf or boiled new potatoes, fairly drenched in butter and scattered with fat flakes of sea salt.

Thai green vegetable curry

Everyone I know extols the virtues of Thai food but my limited experience of it has been pretty dismal (except for once in Sydney and at least that's relatively in the right part of the world). Yet I love all the flavours that are so typical of it: coconut (almost addictively so); coriander; the in-your-face citrusy – some people say soapy – fragrance of lemongrass; and lime must be one of the cleanest, freshest tastes on the planet. I don't go overboard on chilli, I don't have the constitution for it, but it adds the necessary fire. I cannot abide the little ropy pieces of ginger bark that lurk in the sauce and get stuck in your teeth – so I just squeeze the ginger as hard as I can. I have a similar problem with lemongrass, which is why it is important to choose fresh, young stems, remove the outer leaves and then slice it as finely as you can with your very sharpest knife.

SERVES 4
3 tablespoons groundnut oil
250 g/9 oz cauliflower, cut into 4 cm/2 inch florets
250 g/9 oz carrots, peeled, cut in half lengthways, then into half moons on the diagonal, slightly less than 1 cm/½ inch thick
250 g/9 oz courgettes, cut in half lengthways, then into half moons on the diagonal, slightly less than 1 cm/½ inch thick
200 g/7 oz shiitake mushrooms, thickly sliced
400 ml/14 fl oz unsweetened coconut milk
150 ml/5 fl oz vegetable stock, made with bouillon powder
1½ tablespoons tamari
8 Kaffir lime leaves
100 g/3½ oz fine green beans, topped and tailed
small handful of coriander

green curry paste
2 stalks of lemongrass, tough outer leaves removed, the rest chopped very finely
2 shallots, finely diced
juice and zest of 1½ limes
3 green chillies
1 teaspoon ground coriander
1 teaspoon ground cumin
5 garlic cloves
1 bunch of coriander, about 60 g/2 oz
1 dessertspoon Thai seven spice (optional)
4 cm/2 inch piece ginger, grated and squeezed, and the resulting liquid reserved

To make the green curry paste, place all the ingredients in a food processor, ideally in the small herb chopping attachment. Otherwise, do it all by hand, using a very sharp knife or mezzaluna. The quantities above will give you a little more than you actually need, but I found it difficult to process with less. You will need 5 tablespoons of the

mixture, more if you like a hotter version than I do. Any left over can be refrigerated for a couple of weeks or even frozen.

Heat the groundnut oil in a heavy-bottomed saucepan. Add the cauliflower florets. Toss them in the hot oil for 2–3 minutes, until they begin to brown prettily all around and to soften slightly. Add the carrots and repeat the process, then the courgettes. Next add the shiitake mushrooms and sauté for a minute or so. Now add the coconut milk and most of the stock as well as 5 tablespoons of the green curry mixture, the tamari and the Kaffir lime leaves, lightly crushed, but not torn, to release more of their distinctive aroma, then add the green beans.

Simmer for a couple of minutes over a gentle heat, then add the remaining stock. Stir gently for another couple of minutes to allow the flavours to mingle.

Garnish with fresh coriander and serve with basmati rice or Thai jasmine rice.

Pumpkin curry

This, with the creamed coconut, plays on the sweetness of pumpkin while the spices give it a fuller, rounder taste.

SERVES 4
1 tablespoon olive oil
2 large onions, diced
2 garlic cloves, crushed
1 teaspoon ground coriander
2 teaspoons cumin
¼ teaspoon turmeric
1 kg/2 lb 4 oz pumpkin, before trimming and peeling, cut into 2 cm/1 inch chunks
sea salt and freshly ground black pepper
2 red chillies, finely chopped
1 green chilli, finely chopped
3 cm/1½ inch piece of ginger, grated and squeezed, and the resulting liquid reserved
1 tablespoon soft brown or caster sugar
90 g/3 oz creamed coconut
3–4 tomatoes, quartered
3 tablespoons finely chopped fresh coriander
1 tablespoon sesame oil or olive oil
3 tablespoons desiccated coconut

Heat the olive oil in a large saucepan. Add the onions and garlic and fry until translucent.

Add the ground coriander, cumin and turmeric and cook, adding a couple of tablespoons of water to loosen. Then add the pumpkin, a little salt and pepper and sauté for about 10 minutes, until the pumpkin starts to brown slightly and soften.

Add the red and green chillies, reserving a little for garnish. Then add the ginger juice, the sugar and the creamed coconut and stir constantly over a medium heat until the coconut is completely melted.

When the pumpkin is tender but still holding its shape, add the quartered tomatoes and the coriander, stirring gently until the tomatoes are no longer raw.

Finally, stir in the sesame or olive oil and 1 tablespoon of the desiccated coconut. Transfer to a warmed serving dish and garnish with the remaining coconut and chilli. Serve with basmati rice or warmed peshwari naan bread.

Steamed vegetables with a grain mustard dressing

Some people feel they haven't eaten unless there's a piece of flesh on their plate. I don't feel I've eaten unless there's a veritable forest of vegetables on mine. And on days when I've stuffed my face – you know the ones, biscuits, rubbishy chocolate, you name it – at the very least I know I can come home to a plate of these and feel like a human being again. The vitamin hit is practically instant. Vary the vegetables as you wish as long as you keep to the basic principle of hardest ones first, softer ones after. If in a particularly delicate state, eat quite, quite plain and if in need of more sustenance, cook up some Italian organic short grain brown rice. It normally takes 45 minutes to cook to perfection, but cook it in a pressure cooker and it takes about 30. Add some good olive oil, a dash of tamari and Tabasco and a sprinkling of gomasio (pounded sesame seeds and salt) – great for beating free radicals because of the vitamin E in the sesame seeds.

SERVES 2–4
8 small new potatoes, cut in half
2 carrots, cut into thick batons
180 g/6 oz broccoli florets
200 g/7 oz cauliflower florets
1 small head fennel, thinly sliced lengthways
100 g/3½ oz green beans, topped and tailed
1 sweet potato, peeled and sliced (optional)
2 leeks, small and thin, cut in half

dressing
4 tablespoons olive oil
3 dessertspoons grain mustard
3 garlic cloves, crushed
dash of balsamic vinegar
sea salt and freshly ground black pepper

Bring a large pan of water to the boil and place a colander on top, layered up with the vegetables. Start with a layer of potatoes, then carrots, then broccoli and cauliflower, then the fennel, beans and sweet potato, if using, and finally the leeks. Cover with a lid and steam for 10–15 minutes.

Meanwhile, whisk the olive oil into the mustard and garlic until thick, then loosen with a dash of balsamic vinegar. Season to taste with salt and pepper.

Transfer the vegetables to a large plate with the dressing beside.

Green beans with tomatoes and garlic

I think I must have eaten this every week of my life since I was a small child and I never ever tire of it. If you buy the beans in packets, an easy way to trim them is to knock the bag so that all the beans fall to one end, then cut them through the bag, first on one side, then on the other. Mediterranean vegetable dishes do not call for al dente; the softness of a vegetable when it comes as a result of braising in a mixture of oil and stock or sauce, as here – rather than boiling – is an altogether different phenomenon as more of the vegetable's flavour is released and made available.

SERVES 2–4
200 g/7 oz green beans, topped and tailed
4 tablespoons olive oil
1 small red onion, sliced
4 garlic cloves, crushed
5 tomatoes, cut into quarters
sea salt and freshly ground black pepper
dash of Tabasco sauce

Bring a saucepan of salted water to the boil and blanch the beans until they are tender, about 5–7 minutes, then drain.

Heat the oil in a saucepan. Add the onion and garlic and cook until translucent. Add the tomatoes and beans, some salt and pepper and the Tabasco. I like to cook them on quite a high heat and to add the occasional spoonful of water to the pan so as to loosen the juices, but keep adjusting the heat as you see fit, until you have a thick sauce and the beans are very tender.

Mashed potato with wild mushrooms

I think I've gone on quite enough about mushrooms and cream so I'll just get on with it. As for the mashed potato, this is the old-fashioned kind, fluffy and light but with the liberty of olive oil as well as the butter and the milk (or cream if you prefer). I prefer tarragon to thyme in this but it's up to you.

SERVES 4
600 g/1 lb 5 oz floury potatoes, such as King Edward or Kerr's Pink, peeled and
    roughly chopped
60 g/2 oz butter
4 tablespoons milk or double cream
2 tablespoons extra virgin olive oil
sea salt and white pepper

mushrooms
30 g/1 oz butter
2 garlic cloves, finely chopped
2 shallots, finely chopped
200 g/7 oz organic chestnut mushrooms
100 g/3½ oz shiitake mushrooms, sliced
5 tablespoons brandy or Marsala
30 g/1 oz dried porcini mushrooms, just covered with boiling water, a dash of brandy
    and a dash of tamari
125 g/4 oz fresh wild mushrooms
3 tablespoons double cream
1 tablespoon tamari
dash of Tabasco sauce
1 bay leaf
small sprig of tarragon or thyme
1 tablespoon finely chopped flat-leafed parsley

Put the potatoes in a large saucepan of well salted water. Cover, bring to the boil, then turn the heat down to a steady simmer. Continue with the rest of the preparations until they are soft enough to mash.

For the mushrooms, heat the butter in a sauté pan or other deep frying pan. Add the garlic and shallots, a little salt and pepper, and fry until beginning to brown. Add the chestnut and shiitake mushrooms, along with half the brandy or Marsala, and sauté over a medium heat until just cooked. Don't worry if they weep – the liquid will contribute to the sauce. Then add the porcini mushrooms and their strained soaking liquid, followed a minute later by the more delicate wild mushrooms.

Continue frying over a medium to high heat for about 8 minutes, so that there is still a little of the liquid left in the pan. Add the rest of the brandy, lower the heat and let it cook down. Stir in the cream, tamari, Tabasco and the bay leaf and tarragon or thyme and heat to boiling point. Simmer for about 5 more minutes so that all the flavours can work their particular alchemy. Adjust the seasoning with salt and pepper.

Meanwhile, drain the potatoes, mash well and add the butter, milk or cream, olive oil and salt and pepper. Serve on warmed plates with the mushrooms and their sauce, sprinkled with a little chopped parsley. A watercress or chicory salad with a good mustard vinaigrette works perfectly and helps all that richness go down.

Filled courgettes with ricotta and toasted almonds with fresh tomato sauce

I have always adored filled courgettes. My mother makes the most delicate fillings with almonds and raisins, or with finely chopped eggs and parsley, or with things I no longer eat. Not, I have to say, with ricotta, though I made her these one day and she loved them.

SERVES 2–4
2–3 large courgettes (about 500 g/1 lb 2 oz in total), tops cut off
4 tablespoons olive oil
2 shallots, finely chopped
1 garlic clove, crushed
100 g/3½ oz ricotta
1 tablespoon freshly grated Parmesan
½ teaspoon bouillon powder
30 g/1 oz whole almonds, roasted and chopped into thin slivers
2 tablespoons fresh white breadcrumbs
1 tablespoon chopped fresh basil or ½ tablespoon basil, ½ tablespoon chives
sea salt and freshly ground black pepper

sauce
4–6 tablespoons olive oil
2 garlic cloves, finely chopped
1 small red onion, finely diced
500 g/1 lb 2 oz tomatoes, roughly chopped
8 black olives, stoned (optional)
few basil leaves, roughly torn

Cut the courgettes in half and either keep intact and hollow out with an apple corer or slice lengthways and scoop out the insides. Roughly chop the removed courgette flesh.

Heat about half the oil in a saucepan. Add the shallots and garlic and the chopped courgette flesh. Sweat for 6–7 minutes. Stir in the ricotta, Parmesan, bouillon powder, almonds, breadcrumbs and herbs, and season to taste with salt and pepper.

Fill the courgettes into gentle mounds if cut into boats or stand them on one end and fill them from the top if hollowed out. Heat the remaining oil in a griddle pan. Fry the courgettes, turning them from time to time, until softened and charred in places. If they are in boats, focus on the courgette side and flash the tops under a hot grill.

To make the sauce, heat the oil in a frying pan. Add the garlic and onion and sweat until translucent. Add the tomatoes and fry for about 8 minutes. Transfer to a dish and place the hot grilled courgettes on top. Garnish with the olives, if using, and basil leaves.

Filled artichokes with saffron sauce

I have usually made these with fresh artichokes – they hark back to my childhood – but I don't think there'd be any chance of doing them in 30 minutes; canned or frozen ones make a more than acceptable alternative. I first found out about frozen artichoke bottoms from Claudia Roden – if they are good enough for her, they are good enough for me.

Matzo meal is available in most large supermarkets – look for the Kosher section. Alternatively, a couple of matzo crackers, finely ground up in a coffee or herb mill, are the same thing. If all else fails, substitute ground water biscuits.

SERVES 2–4
1 can artichoke bottoms (they usually contain 5)
half a lemon
4–6 tablespoons saffron stock, made with a few strands of saffron and hot water
1 tablespoon olive oil
1 garlic clove, finely sliced

filling
few saffron strands, soaked in 150 ml/5 fl oz hot bouillon
75 g/2½ oz ground almonds and fine matzo meal, mixed in equal proportions
1 large egg, raw
1 boiled egg, roughly chopped
1 spring onion, green part, sliced
1 medium tomato, diced
1 tablespoon olive oil
dash of Tabasco sauce
1 teaspoon chopped fresh coriander
1 teaspoon chopped fresh parsley
½ teaspoon harissa
½ whole nutmeg, grated
2 garlic cloves, crushed
sea salt and freshly ground black pepper

sauce
8 or so saffron strands soaked in 250 ml/8 fl oz hot stock, made with ½ teaspoon
    bouillon powder
2–3 garlic cloves, crushed or finely sliced
1 teaspoon lemon juice
300 ml/10 fl oz double cream
1 tablespoon finely chopped fresh parsley or chives

Preheat the oven to 190°C/375°F/gas 5. Rinse the artichoke bottoms in cold water to rid them of their briny taste as much as possible, then rub them with the halved lemon.

Bring the saffron stock, olive oil and garlic to the boil in a heavy-bottomed saucepan. Add the artichoke bottoms and reduce to a simmer. Continue to cook gently until the liquid is reduced and there is a small amount of golden saffron sauce coating the artichokes; this will take 5–7 minutes.

Mix all the filling ingredients together and fill the artichoke bottoms. Transfer to an ovenproof dish with any remaining sauce and an extra spoonful of saffron stock or water drizzled over if it looks dry.

Cover with a lid or foil and bake for 10 minutes, basting at least once. The filling should remain moist, though you can remove the lid and bake them for a further 3–4 minutes to turn them pale gold on top.

To make the sauce, heat the saffron stock and boil until reduced by about half. Add the garlic, lemon juice and cream. Cook over a low heat for 5–7 minutes, then add whichever herb you are using.

To serve, place the artichokes on a serving plate and spoon the hot sauce all around.

(If you want a more Mediterranean feel, serve with the tomato sauce as made with the Filled courgettes on page 148 instead of the cream and saffron sauce and bake the artichokes in the sauce.)

Filled cabbage with colcannon

Many people tell me that they hardly ever cook English vegetables any more – not cabbage or carrots or cauliflower. This is a great shame, especially in the winter. A whole Savoy takes only 15 minutes to cook – or 10 in a pressure cooker.

SERVES 4
1 Savoy cabbage, 3 large outer leaves removed and shredded
2 large potatoes, roughly chopped
2 tablespoons groundnut oil
2 onions, diced
6 garlic cloves, finely sliced
400 g/14 oz can chopped tomatoes
250 g/9 oz ricotta
200 g/7 oz Cheddar, grated
15 g/½ oz butter
pinch of freshly grated nutmeg
1½ tablespoons grain mustard
5 tablespoons double cream
1 egg, beaten
sea salt and freshly ground black pepper
60 g/2 oz breadcrumbs (optional)
30 g/1 oz hazelnuts or other nuts, coarsely chopped (optional)

Bring a large saucepan of salted water to the boil and cook the whole cabbage for 10–15 minutes. At the same time, put the potatoes in another pan of salted water, bring to the boil and cook until tender.

Meanwhile, heat the oil in a frying pan. Add the onions and garlic and sauté until translucent. Remove half of the onion and garlic mixture to a second frying pan. Add the tomatoes to the first frying pan and simmer for about 10 minutes.

Drain the potatoes and set aside. Add the shredded cabbage leaves to the second frying pan and fry for a minute, until the cabbage is wilted. Then mash the potatoes and add the cabbage, along with the ricotta, about a third of the grated Cheddar, the butter, nutmeg, mustard, cream and egg. Season to taste with salt and pepper, and mix together.

Drain the boiled cabbage very well. Open out the leaves while keeping them attached at the base. Generously fill in between the leaves with the potato and cheese mixture.

Preheat the grill. Pour the tomato sauce into a heatproof dish. Place the cabbage on top. Mix together the remaining grated cheese, breadcrumbs and nuts, if using, and sprinkle over the cabbage. Flash under the hot grill for a few minutes. Serve at once, cut into wedges, discarding the hard central core as you cut.

Griddled peppers
with cannellini beans, feta and black olives

Filled peppers have always represented the nadir of vegetarian cooking to me and I avoided them like the plague for years. I won't dwell on the negative but will remind you of the very great difference that grilling or charring makes. Instead of baking them for ages so that the skin hangs off in indigestible, flaccid strips, you need to give them the burn – whether you eat the black bits is up to you, but make sure that the flesh is soft and just so – not squidgy, not hard. The filling must be super fresh, full of texture, colour, flavour. I used the long thin Romero peppers because they are so very sweet and because their elongated shape dispels that old image of filled peppers, standing to attention all squeezed together in a dish.

SERVES 2–4
2 red peppers, ideally Romero
200 g/7 oz feta cheese, cut into finger-length strips
200 g/7 oz canned cannellini beans, drained weight
16 kalamata olives
1 tablespoon chopped fresh parsley or coriander
1 spring onion, very finely sliced
1 stick of celery, very finely sliced (optional)
1 tomato, deseeded and chopped small
1 garlic clove, finely chopped or crushed
3–4 tablespoons olive oil
juice of half a lemon
sea salt and freshly ground black pepper
1 tablespoon pine nuts or almonds, lightly toasted and chopped into slivers to garnish

Blacken the peppers over a fierce flame, holding them by the tail and turning them over swiftly to cover all aspects. Cut them in half and allow to cool briefly on a plate, catching and reserving the sweet juices.

Mix all the remaining ingredients except the nuts, adding salt and pepper to taste. Loosely pile into each half pepper, drizzling the juices all over and sprinkling with the nuts. Serve with a pile of rocket leaves and a side dish of harissa or chermoula (page 17) for those that like it.

Carefree couscous, risotto and other 30-minute feasts Think how happy you'd be if you could bring out not just a quick snack or salad but a whole feast in 30 minutes. Collect your ingredients, take a moment to breathe first, follow the order of preparation and go for it.

Saffron braised carrots with broad bean pilaf

If you can, find a bunch of small organic carrots with the green tops left on. They are quite delicate except, perhaps, for the stalks, which can remain tough even after braising. The rice pilaf is perfect here and with any of the Moroccan pulse or vegetable dishes in this book.

SERVES 4
500 g/1 lb 2 oz bunched carrots
4 tablespoons olive oil
1 teaspoon ground cumin
generous pinch of saffron
150 ml/5 fl oz water
½ teaspoon bouillon powder
4 large or 6 small garlic cloves
dash of Tabasco sauce
sea salt and freshly ground black pepper
lemon wedges

pilaf
250 g/9 oz basmati rice
200 g/7 oz broad beans
2 tablespoons olive oil
3 large shallots, finely sliced
2 garlic cloves, finely sliced
1 teaspoon cumin seeds
2 tablespoons plump raisins
1 tablespoon pine nuts

Wash the carrots thoroughly, paying particular attention to the tops. If they are large carrots, cut them in half lengthways but leave them attached at the top.

Place the carrots in a large saucepan together with all the other ingredients except for the lemon wedges. Cover with a lid and simmer over a medium heat for about 20 minutes, until the carrots are tender and coated in the saffron and garlic sauce.

Meanwhile, put the rice in a saucepan and cover with its volume in water. Cover with a lid, bring to the boil, then reduce to a simmer for about 12 minutes, until the water is absorbed and the rice pockmarked when you lift the lid.

While the rice cooks, blanch the broad beans in boiling water for about 7 minutes and drain. Heat the olive oil in a saucepan. Add the shallots and fry until brown and crisp in places. Add the garlic and cumin seeds and fry for another 2–3 minutes. Add the broad beans and keep over a low heat. When the rice is cooked, add it to the broad beans. Stir well over a low heat for a minute, adding the raisins and pine nuts, and serve with the carrots.

Couscous with green olives and preserved lemon

The preserved lemon of the title is, I admit, aspirational. You may find them in a Middle Eastern shop or you could make your own (page 17); use three or four pieces of preserved lemon in place of the fresh one in the recipe. Even a small lemon makes this slightly bitter, so use half if you're afraid. Toasting the almonds adds flavour and a crunchier texture. Allow them to cool before adding them in or they'll go a bit soft. Here is another opportunity to bring out your harissa or chermoula.

SERVES 4
2 tablespoons olive oil
1 large onion, thinly sliced
1 whole head of garlic, peeled, cloves left whole
1 small lemon, cut into eight
2 x 350 g/12 oz jars of stoned green olives, drained
200 ml/7 fl oz vegetable stock, made with a good pinch
**   of bouillon powder and a few saffron stalks**
pinch of paprika
50 g/1½ oz whole almonds, blanched and peeled

COUSCOUS
400 g/14 oz couscous
400 ml/14 fl oz hot vegetable stock, made with 1 teaspoon
**   of bouillon powder**
1 tablespoon butter or olive oil

Preheat the oven to its highest setting.

Put the couscous in a bowl and cover with the hot stock. Add the butter or oil. Stir once and set aside.

Heat the olive oil in a frying pan. Add the onion and fry until golden brown.

Add the garlic, lemon and olives. Cover with the stock, add a pinch of paprika, stir, and bring to the boil for 5 minutes, then lower the heat and simmer until the stock is well reduced, about 10–12 minutes.

Meanwhile, toast the almonds in the oven for 4 minutes – don't let them burn. Add them to the olives for the last 2 minutes of cooking time. By this time the garlic will be completely soft and the sauce still runny but not watery.

Serve at once with the couscous and a dish of harissa or chermoula and/or a bowl of Greek yoghurt.

Algerian couscous
with chickpeas in tomato and cumin broth

Do you want to eat this the authentic way? Then take a little couscous in the palm of your hand. Place a chickpea or raisin in it and roll into a small ball. Then (are you ready for this?) flick the ball with your thumb into your open mouth!

SERVES 4
3 tablespoons olive oil
500 g/1 lb 2 oz leeks, trimmed and chopped into 2 cm/1 inch pieces
275 g/10 oz onion, finely chopped
4 garlic cloves, sliced
sea salt and freshly ground black pepper
3 tablespoons ground cumin
pinch of saffron in about 3 tablespoons hot water
500 g/1 lb 2 oz carrots, cut into 2 cm/1 inch thick chunks
500 g/1 lb 2 oz courgettes, cut into 2 cm/1 inch thick chunks
400 g/14 oz can chickpeas, liquid included
400 ml/14 fl oz can tomatoes (not chopped), liquid included
2 tablespoons raisins
1 tablespoon chopped parsley to garnish

COUSCOUS
400 g/14 oz couscous
400 ml/14 fl oz hot vegetable stock, made with 1 teaspoon of bouillon powder
1 tablespoon butter or olive oil

Cover the couscous with the hot stock. Add the butter or oil. Stir once and set aside.

Heat the oil in a large heavy-bottomed saucepan. Add the leeks and sauté until golden. Remove and set aside. In the same pan, add the onion and fry over a medium heat until just browned. Add the garlic and some salt, then add the cumin and cook for a further 3–4 minutes, loosening with a little of the saffron water.

Add the carrots and sauté until just beginning to soften. Add the courgettes and sauté for a further couple of minutes. Then add the sautéed leeks, the chickpeas, the tomatoes and the rest of the saffron water. Finally, stir in the raisins.

Simmer for about 10 minutes, until the vegetables are tender, even soft, but not soggy. If the sauce seems too thick – it should be more of a broth than a sauce – add a little more hot water. Season with salt and pepper to taste and sprinkle the chopped parsley on top.

Serve with the couscous, with harissa or chermoula (page 17) on the side.

Porcini risotto

The thing about risotto is this: you can stand over it, judiciously adding your stock and stirring all the while for a full 20–25 minutes, but my friend Anjalika, who cooks like a dream, doesn't. After the first couple of ladlefuls of stock are absorbed by the rice she adds a little more, then gets on with preparing whatever else she is serving. Occasionally she adds another ladleful of stock and gives it a gentle stir, until the last of the stock is absorbed and the grains of rice are creamily cooked, adding a final glug of extra virgin olive oil. Hardly slaving over a hot stove, is it? For the cook in a tearing hurry, it's worth noting that vialone nano rice cooks faster than arborio, taking only about 15 minutes.

SERVES 4
50 g/1½ oz dried porcini mushrooms
1 teaspoon bouillon powder
3 tablespoons brandy
1 teaspoon tamari
2 garlic cloves, finely sliced
50 g/1½ oz butter or 3 tablespoons olive oil
6 shallots, finely chopped
350 g/12 oz vialone nano or other risotto rice
sea salt and freshly ground black pepper
90 g/3 oz Parmesan, grated
handful of fresh parsley, chopped

Place the dried porcini in a bowl with a pinch of the bouillon powder, the brandy, tamari, 1 of the sliced garlic cloves and 350 ml/12 fl oz of hot water. Soak until the porcini are just soft, remembering that they are going to soften some more during cooking.

Meanwhile, put the remaining bouillon powder into a measuring jug and add 650 ml/ 1¼ pints of hot water. Set aside.

Melt the butter, or heat the olive oil, in a heavy-bottomed saucepan. Add the shallots and the remaining garlic and fry until translucent. Then add the rice and stir frequently over a medium heat until it too becomes translucent. Strain the mushroom soaking liquid and add to the rice. Season with salt and pepper. Gradually add 250 ml/9 fl oz of the stock, stirring all the time until the liquid is incorporated.

Add the mushrooms and then gradually add the remaining stock, stirring until the liquid is absorbed. The risotto will be very dark, the rice creamy, yet the grains still separate.

Stir in about half the Parmesan, scatter over the parsley and serve at once. Serve the remaining Parmesan separately. I would also serve a bowl of spinach, wilted and with a light dressing of olive oil.

Saffron risotto

It's always worth keeping a little stash of saffron threads, wrapped in waxed paper inside a little box, somewhere cool and dark. I've lost count of the number of times I've turned the simplest of dishes into something suddenly exotic and divine – think of Saffron potato, spinach and Fontina cheese pie on page 120. Olive oil may be the liquid gold of the Italians, but saffron is the gold – 24 carat – of the Levant. I love simple, elegant, sophisticated food like this. It makes life worth living.

SERVES 4

1.5 litres/2½ pints vegetable stock, made with bouillon powder
3 tablespoons olive oil or 50 g/1½ oz butter, plus a little extra of either to serve
2 shallots, very finely diced
350 g/12 oz vialone nano or other risotto rice
180 ml/6 fl oz wine, red or white
½ teaspoon saffron strands, crushed to a powder in a pestle and mortar, plus a few
    extra strands to add at the end of cooking
75 g/2½ oz Parmesan, freshly grated
sea salt and freshly ground black pepper

Bring the stock to a very low simmer in a saucepan and keep at a low simmer as you cook the risotto.

Heat 2 tablespoons of the oil or melt 30 g/1 oz of the butter in a heavy-bottomed saucepan. Add the shallots and fry until soft and translucent. Then add the rice and stir frequently over a medium heat until it too becomes translucent. Add the wine and a ladleful of hot stock and bring to the boil, stirring constantly.

When nearly all the liquid is absorbed, add about a quarter of the remaining stock. Cook at a steady lively simmer until it is nearly all absorbed and then add another ladleful. Stir, and when that is absorbed, add another.

About halfway through the cooking – about 10 minutes – add the saffron powder, dissolved in a little hot stock.

Continue to add the hot stock little by little, stirring gently whenever you can, until the rice is cooked and creamy, yet with its grains still separate. Finally, add the extra saffron strands. These will really bring out the saffron flavour.

Remove from the heat and stir in half the Parmesan. Put a lid on the pan and let the risotto rest for 1 minute while the cheese melts. Then give it a final vigorous stir, an extra slug of olive oil or a small knob of butter, season with salt and pepper, and serve with the rest of the Parmesan on the side.

Carrot and thyme risotto

A pan with rounded sides is ideal so that the risotto doesn't stick in the corners but any heavy-bottomed pan is fine.

Fresh thyme lifts this risotto into something gloriously, irresistibly aromatic. Just a word of advice: never reheat a risotto – it just doesn't. If you have any left over, make it into fritters or a frittata (page 67) the next day.

SERVES 4
30 g/1 oz unsalted butter
1 tablespoon olive oil (or 3 tablespoons olive oil and omit the butter)
6 shallots, finely chopped
2 garlic cloves, crushed
500 g/1 lb 2 oz carrots, thickly sliced
small bunch of thyme
350 g/12 oz vialone nano or other risotto rice
1 litre/1¾ pints hot vegetable stock, made with 1 teaspoon bouillon powder
sea salt and freshly ground black pepper
4 tablespoons freshly grated Parmesan, plus extra to serve

Heat the butter and oil – or just the oil – in a heavy-bottomed saucepan. Add the shallots and garlic and fry until translucent. Then add the carrots and sauté gently until they begin to soften slightly, then add about half the thyme.

Now add the rice and stir over a low heat until it becomes translucent.

Add the hot stock, a couple of ladlefuls at a time, stirring frequently until all the stock is absorbed and the rice is creamy – this will take about 20 minutes. By this time the carrots will have become softer still, and the risotto will have a gentle orange glow. The carrots should still be in discernible chunks though, so don't let them oversoften initially.

Stir in most of the remaining thyme and season with salt and pepper. I would be tempted to stir in all the Parmesan and to serve extra Parmesan on the side for those who like a really cheesy risotto.

I also like to add a drizzle of extra virgin olive oil on top, but this, like the extra Parmesan, is optional. Garnish with a few thyme leaves.

Fennel risotto

The fennel imparts its subtle flavour to the rice and becomes meltingly soft as the risotto cooks. This risotto is also delicious with a handful of blanched petits pois added towards the end of the cooking time.

SERVES 4
2 tablespoons light olive oil
3 shallots, finely diced
1 stick of celery, finely sliced (optional)
2 garlic cloves, finely sliced
300 g/11 oz vialone nano or other risotto rice
1.25 litres/2 pints hot vegetable stock, made with 1 teaspoon bouillon powder
2 fennel bulbs, roughly chopped, green fronds removed
6 tablespoons dry white wine
50 g/1½ oz Parmesan, freshly grated
sea salt and freshly ground black pepper

Heat the oil in a large heavy-bottomed saucepan. Add the shallots and celery, if using, and sauté until translucent. Add the garlic and continue to fry for a couple of minutes without allowing it to brown.

Add the rice and stir over a low heat until it becomes translucent.

Add a ladleful of the hot stock and stir constantly until the liquid is fully absorbed. Add the fennel, half the wine and another ladleful of stock. Stir frequently, adding a ladleful of stock at a time. Though you might not need to stir the whole time, it is important that you only add a little more stock when the previous lot is absorbed. Add the remaining wine along with the last of the stock.

Remove from the heat and stir in half the Parmesan. Put a lid on the pan and let the risotto rest for 1 minute while the cheese melts. Then give it a final vigorous stir, season with salt and pepper to taste and serve the rest of the Parmesan separately.

Puy lentils with griddled vegetables

Pressure cooker time: if you haven't got one it will, I am afraid, take a good 45 minutes until the lentils reach a state of perfect tenderness.

SERVES 2–4
4 tablespoons olive oil, plus extra to serve
1 small red onion, cut into chunks
1 whole head of garlic, cloves peeled and finely sliced
400 g/14 oz Puy lentils
2 bay leaves
1 tablespoon tamari
2 tablespoons balsamic vinegar
2 large handfuls of basil, roughly torn
1 handful of parsley, finely chopped
sea salt and freshly ground black pepper

vegetables
1 red pepper, deseeded, pith removed and cut into 8 strips
1 large courgette, cut into 2 cm/1 inch chunks
1 fennel bulb, cut lengthways into 8 pieces
1 aubergine, sliced about ½ cm/¼ inch thick
1 red onion, cut into quarters
1–2 tablespoons olive oil
1 garlic clove, finely chopped or crushed
dash of balsamic vinegar
dash of Tabasco sauce

Heat half the olive oil in a pressure cooker pan. Add the onion and garlic and sauté until translucent. Add the lentils, 1 litre/1¾ pints of water and the bay leaves. Cover with the lid and bring to the boil. Reduce the heat and cook under pressure for 25 minutes.

Meanwhile, baste the vegetables in the olive oil.

Heat a griddle. Griddle the vegetables until they are nicely striped. When they are ready, season with the garlic, balsamic vinegar, Tabasco, a little salt and pepper and any remaining olive oil.

Once the lentils are cooked, season them with tamari, balsamic vinegar, the remaining 2 tablespoons of olive oil, the basil, chopped parsley and salt and pepper to taste. Spoon on to plates and serve with an abundance of griddled vegetables over each and more olive oil drizzled over if you wish.

Coconut dahl
with raita, cardamom rice and paneer tikka

It's a bit of a nerve putting a whole Indian meal in a fast food book, but I swear it can be done. I like my dahl very smooth, not quite a soup but almost. Marinating the paneer – a mild white Indian cheese – overnight will speed things up substantially and is easy to do when you get in the swing of producing meals on a regular basis. It's the sort of thing you can do while the ads are on and you're making yourself a cup of tea.

SERVES 4–6
3 tablespoons sunflower oil
1 onion, diced
2 garlic cloves, sliced
1 teaspoon black mustard seeds
1 tablespoon ground cumin
1 tablespoon ground coriander
1 tablespoon garam masala
about 4 cm/2 inches of ginger, grated and squeezed, and the resulting liquid reserved
1 small potato, peeled and cubed
1 stick of celery, sliced thinly
1 carrot, cut into 2 cm/1 inch pieces
1 litre/1¾ pints vegetable stock, made with ½ teaspoon bouillon powder
250 g/9 oz red lentils
50 g/1½ oz creamed coconut
1 tablespoon roughly chopped fresh coriander, plus a small handful for garnish
2 tablespoons raisins
4 small dry red chillies or 1 bird's eye chilli, chopped very finely, or ¼ teaspoon dried chilli powder
30 g/1 oz desiccated coconut (optional)
250 g/9 oz tender young spinach, washed
2 tomatoes, quartered

paneer tikka
3 tablespoons Greek yoghurt
3 tablespoons shop-bought tikka paste
225 g/8 oz paneer, cut into cubes

cardamom rice
1 tablespoon groundnut oil
1 small onion, diced
375 g/13 oz basmati rice
6 cardamom pods, left whole
small piece of mace (optional)

raita
500 ml/18 fl oz Greek yoghurt
1 cucumber, coarsely grated, salted and left to drain
4 garlic cloves, crushed
1 teaspoon tamarind paste, to garnish (optional)

For the paneer tikka, mix the yoghurt with the tikka paste and gently mix in the cubed paneer. Ideally, marinate for several hours or overnight, but it's not the end of the world if you haven't.

Preheat the oven to its highest setting. Roast the marinated paneer in the hot oven for 15–20 minutes.

Heat the oil in a heavy-bottomed saucepan. Add the onion and garlic and fry until translucent. Add all the spices and the ginger juice and continue to fry, stirring all the time until the spices become a little darker.

Then, while continuing to stir, add the potato, celery and carrot and about 100 ml/ 3½ fl oz of the stock. Remove a couple of tablespoons of the mixture to a separate bowl and reserve, then add the lentils to the saucepan and keep stirring. Add the rest of the stock and bring to the boil. Then cover, reduce the heat to a gentle simmer and cook until it all softens to a purée, about 15–20 minutes.

Return the reserved mixture to the saucepan, together with the creamed coconut, chopped coriander, raisins, chilli and desiccated coconut, if using. Then add the spinach, pushing it down into the pot and stirring until it is wilted. Finally, add the tomato quarters so they soften in the heat.

While the dahl is cooking, cook the cardamom rice. Heat the oil in a heavy-bottomed saucepan. Add the diced onion and fry until pale gold. Add the rice and stir until translucent. Pour enough water over it to cover by 2 cm/1 inch and bring to the boil. Add the cardamom pods and the piece of mace, if using. Cover with a lid and reduce to a simmer. After about 12 minutes the rice should be perfectly cooked and fluffy.

While they are all cooking away, prepare the raita. Mix together all but the tamarind, if using, and just swirl that on top.

Serve with some warmed naan bread, chutney or pickle, and the raita on the side. Add a sprig of coriander to each serving.

A vegetarian paella worth staying in for

If you can't find quick-cook brown rice, then use short grain white or proper paella rice. Long grain rice, white or brown, just doesn't have the plumpness you need. I've said the peppers should be small. If they can't be, use only half of each and if that seems like an inconvenience, stick to one colour.

SERVES 4

300 g/11 oz quick-cook brown rice
1 tablespoon tamari, plus 1 teaspoon
4 tablespoons olive oil
2 tablespoons paprika
2 tablespoons ground cumin
5 garlic cloves, crushed
200 ml/7 fl oz hot vegetable stock, made with a small pinch of bouillon powder and a pinch of saffron stalks
3 tablespoons white wine
½ teaspoon Tabasco sauce
125 g/4 oz carrots, peeled and sliced ½ cm/¼ inch thick
125 g/4 oz courgettes, sliced ½ cm/¼ inch thick
150 g/5 oz petits pois
1 corn on the cob, stripped
1 small red pepper, deseeded, pith removed and cut into 8 strips
1 small yellow pepper, deseeded, pith removed and cut into 8 strips
6 sun-dried tomatoes in oil, drained
12 black olives, stoned
sea salt and freshly ground black pepper
1 tablespoon chopped flat-leafed parsley

Place the rice and 450 ml/16 fl oz of water in a large saucepan or, ideally, a pressure cooker, as this will speed things up. Add 1 teaspoon tamari to the water. Cover, bring to the boil, then reduce the heat and, if in a pressure cooker, cook for 15 minutes. Otherwise, follow packet instructions. There should be no trace of chalkiness but the rice must not be soggy. Remember that the rice will soften very slightly when you fry it with the vegetables.

Meanwhile, heat 3 tablespoons of olive oil in your largest sauté pan, frying pan or wok. Add the paprika and cumin, stir, and fry for a minute. Then add the garlic, stir, and fry for a minute. Now slowly add tablespoons of the hot stock as well as the wine, stirring between additions, until you've used about half the liquid and the spices form a thin paste in the pan. Now stir in the Tabasco.

Add the carrots, stirring until coated in the sauce, then fry for a couple of minutes. Next, add the courgettes, stirring until coated in the sauce. Then add the petits pois and corn

kernels. Sauté for a few minutes until the vegetables are tender but still firm. Remove from the heat.

Meanwhile, baste the red and yellow pepper strips in the remaining olive oil. Fry in a griddle pan until charred in places. Set aside.

When the rice is cooked, remove from the heat and, if you used a pressure cooker, allow the pot to lose pressure.

Place the vegetable pan over a low heat. Add the rice, stirring continuously. If it's at all dry add the remaining stock as necessary. Then add the sun-dried tomatoes and black olives and stir for a minute or so. Finally, season, stir in the chopped parsley and cover with the peppers. Serve in the pan as is.

Quick roasts and gratins The beauty of these recipes, with their Pacific and Mediterranean influences, is that, after an initial burst of activity, most of them can then be left alone while you do one of the following: help the children with their homework; clean up; your nails; collapse.

Roasted portobello mushrooms
with herb pesto and soft rocket polenta

You've only 30 minutes remember, so the polenta is the quick-cooking kind, which can be delicious – promise. It will be softer, less textural than the proper, slow cooking type, but the only way to approach these substitutions and shortcuts is not to compare but to give the very best flavour to the ingredients you have the time and budget for. Sometimes the attention and handling is all, even if that's not a very fashionable thing to say.

SERVES 4
1 tablespoon tamari
1 tablespoon brandy
1 tablespoon dry red wine
dash of Tabasco sauce
4 large portobello or field mushrooms
large handful of basil leaves
4 tablespoons olive oil
2 garlic cloves, crushed

polenta
1 litre/1¾ pints vegetable stock made with ½ teaspoon bouillon powder
180 g/6 oz five-minute polenta
5 tablespoons extra virgin olive oil
30 g/1 oz Parmesan, freshly grated
50 g/1½ oz rocket, torn

to serve
1 tablespoon pine nuts (optional)
1 garlic clove, crushed
250 g/9 oz Swiss chard, tough stalks removed and leaves torn
knob of butter
sea salt and freshly ground black pepper

Preheat the oven to 200°C/400°F/gas 6.

Mix together the tamari, brandy, red wine, Tabasco and 1 tablespoon of water and use to baste the mushrooms. Set aside.

Meanwhile, make a mock pesto by putting the basil leaves in a herb chopper or small blender, together with the olive oil and garlic. Season with salt and pepper and blend until fairly fine. Coat the mushrooms with the pesto on both sides, pushing it into the gills as much as you can and reserving any that you do not use.

Put the mushrooms in a roasting tin in the hot oven for about 20 minutes, until they are cooked through and have wept their deep dark liquor.

About 5 minutes before the mushrooms are ready, place the pine nuts, if using, on a baking sheet in the oven to roast.

To cook the Swiss chard, melt the butter in a large saucepan and sweat the garlic. Add the chard. Cover with a lid and cook until wilted, stirring a couple of times to make sure it is well coated in the butter.

Meanwhile, make the polenta. Bring the stock to the boil in a large saucepan. Pour in the polenta in a steady stream. Stir with a wooden spoon until thickened but still quite sloppy. Stir in the olive oil and Parmesan and season to taste with salt and pepper. Finally stir in the torn rocket leaves and transfer to four warmed deep plates.

Place a roasted mushroom on each plate, with any remaining pesto and the juices from the roasting pan poured in as a gravy. Serve the Swiss chard on the side, sprinkled with the roasted pine nuts.

'I love to use the very best ingredients, the freshest possible produce, but sometimes the handling is all'

Roasted new potatoes with garlic fromage frais

I include these because I normally think of roast potatoes in the way most people do: roasts, Sundays or, when I was growing up, always Friday nights. At any rate, a major, sit-down, all-the-works kind of a meal. And don't they always take at least an hour to cook? So here are some you can enjoy in half an hour of doing practically nothing.

SERVES 2–4
100 ml/3½ fl oz olive oil
700 g/about 1½ lb small new potatoes, scrubbed and cut in half lengthways
 if necessary
sea salt

fromage frais
2 garlic cloves, crushed
250 g/9 oz fromage frais
small handful of chives, finely snipped

Preheat the oven to its highest setting. Put the olive oil in a roasting tin and place this in the oven so the oil is hot when the potatoes go into it.

Meanwhile, prepare the potatoes and sprinkle generously with sea salt. Roast for about 25 minutes, until they are browned and tender.

While the potatoes are roasting, mix the crushed garlic with the fromage frais and the snipped chives.

Serve the potatoes piping hot, with the fromage frais in a separate dish.

Roasted sweet potatoes, butternut squash, baby potatoes and shallots with fresh mango

If really pressed for time, you do not need to peel the sweet potatoes, nor of course, the new ones. You can make life easier still by first blanching the shallots in boiling water – hardly longer than a minute so they don't lose flavour. They'll be ten times easier to peel and will save your eyes. Serve with a blanched head of broccoli, generously doused with melted butter, sea salt, freshly ground black pepper and, if you like, a crushed clove of garlic. A big bowl of wilted spinach bound with a little double cream or Greek yoghurt, similarly seasoned, would also do very nicely.

SERVES 4
1 teaspoon tamari
3 tablespoons olive oil
dash of Tabasco sauce
1 tablespoon tamarind paste
4 sweet potatoes, scrubbed and cut into slices less than 1 cm/½ inch thick
1 smallish butternut squash, peeled, seeds removed, then cut into chunks
16 or so small new potatoes, cut in half or sliced if necessary
16 or so shallots, blanched and peeled
1 large or 2 small perfectly ripe, sweet mangoes
4–8 whole garlic cloves, unpeeled
2 tablespoons pumpkin seeds, shelled (optional)
sea salt
sprig of coriander, chopped, for garnish

Preheat the oven to its highest setting. Place a roasting tin in the oven to heat up while you get on with your preparations.

In a large bowl, mix together the tamari, olive oil, Tabasco and half the tamarind paste. Add the chopped vegetables, mangoes and garlic and toss with your hands (or a wooden spoon if you're not the type). Tip the vegetables into the hot roasting tin and roast for 20 minutes. Check now and again to make sure nothing is burning or drying out too much. If necessary, add a drop or two of water or stock or even brandy to keep the vegetables moist. A couple of minutes before the end of the cooking time add the remaining tamarind paste.

Meanwhile, place the pumpkin seeds, if using, in a heavy-bottomed pan with a little crushed sea salt and toast in the oven until they begin to brown and some begin to pop.

Serve the roasted vegetables in warmed plates, sprinkled with the pumpkin seeds and chopped coriander.

Roasted butternut squash
with tofu, green beans and walnuts

This method of cooking tofu is great if you have not had time to marinate it. I have also made this with slices of Golden Cross goat's cheese and poured maple syrup on top of it – a revelatory mixture of sharpness and sweetness.

SERVES 2–4
1 tablespoon olive oil, plus a little extra
dash of Tabasco sauce
sea salt and freshly ground black pepper
1 good-sized butternut squash, about 900 g/2 lb, seeds removed, cut into 8 segments
2–4 garlic cloves, unpeeled
2 small red onions, cut into quarters
150 g/5 oz green beans, topped and tailed
1 teaspoon tamari
30 g/1 oz whole almonds, chopped into slivers
1 tablespoon maple syrup (optional)

tofu
2 tablespoons olive oil
275 g/10 oz tofu, cubed
2 tablespoons tamari

Preheat the oven to its highest setting.

Mix together 1 tablespoon of the olive oil, the Tabasco and a little salt and pepper. Put the butternut squash, garlic and onion quarters in a roasting tin and baste them with the olive oil mixture. Tuck the onion and garlic among the squash so that they don't burn. Roast for 25 minutes, until browned and tender.

Meanwhile, bring a small saucepan of salted water to the boil with a little olive oil. Add the beans and boil for 7 minutes. Drain and refresh under cold water. Set aside.

To prepare the tofu, heat the oil in a small saucepan. Add the tofu and fry for a minute over a high heat, then add the tamari, reduce the heat slightly and continue to fry on all sides until the tofu is well browned all over and crisp in places. It will stick to the bottom of the pan but that is how it cooks best. Use a metal spatula or spoon to turn it over carefully. The tofu will take about 10 minutes to cook.

About 7 minutes before the vegetables are ready, sprinkle them with the tamari, almonds and the green beans, as well as the maple syrup, if using. Return to the oven. The almonds should crisp and caramelize slightly in the maple syrup. Serve the tofu on top of the roasted vegetables, with a crisp green salad on the side.

Jerusalem artichokes with red wine and Gruyère

I usually make this in a heavy, lidded casserole and bake for 40–45 minutes, until the artichokes are soft to melting point. For the sake of speed and efficiency, I've braised them to completion instead. They are absolutely divine like this. Sweet, complex and sophisticated. Adding the Gruyère brings out their sweet nuttiness, but I am as happy with or without it.

SERVES 2

450 g/1 lb Jerusalem artichokes, scrubbed clean, peeled if necessary, and cut very thin (somewhere between a 10p and a £1 coin)
2 generous tablespoons extra virgin olive oil
3–4 garlic cloves, finely sliced
half a bird's eye chilli, very finely chopped
½ teaspoon bouillon powder
1 tablespoon light soy sauce or tamari
sea salt and freshly ground black pepper
50 ml/2 fl oz red (or white) wine
4 or 5 chestnut mushrooms, sliced
50 g/1½ oz Gruyère, grated (optional)
1 tablespoon finely chopped parsley or chives

Place the Jerusalem artichoke slices in a large frying pan, together with the olive oil, garlic, chilli, bouillon powder, soy sauce or tamari, a little salt, the wine and about 100 ml/3½ fl oz of water. Bring to the boil, cover with a lid, then reduce the heat and simmer for about 20 minutes.

After about 10 minutes, turn them over, add the mushrooms and remove the lid so the Jerusalem artichokes are gently browned on both sides and the sauce is well reduced.

Meanwhile, preheat the grill to high.

When the Jerusalem artichokes are ready – that is, just going floppy and with no crunch left to them – sprinkle the Gruyère, if using, on top and flash under the hot grill for a couple of minutes. To serve, sprinkle with the chopped herbs and some freshly ground black pepper.

Braised fennel gratin

I have an unending passion for fennel. Even here, where it is covered in cream, I feel sure that its digestive properties shine through. Braising is a two-way process – the taste of the vegetables into the sauce, the sauce flavour into the vegetables – and the result so much greater than the sum of its parts. A peppery leafed green salad and some warm bread are all you really need for a simple and elegant meal.

SERVES 2
2 fennel bulbs, cut in half lengthways
2 garlic cloves, finely sliced
5 tablespoons light olive oil, plus a little extra
300 ml/10 fl oz hot vegetable stock, made with ½ teaspoon bouillon powder
60 g/2 oz chestnut mushrooms, finely sliced (optional)
dash of tamari for the mushrooms
100 ml/3½ fl oz double cream
30 g/1oz Parmesan, grated

Put the fennel and garlic in a heavy-bottomed frying pan and cover with the olive oil and stock. Bring to the boil, reduce the heat to low and simmer gently for 10–12 minutes or until the fennel is tender and the liquid reduced by three-quarters.

Meanwhile, sauté the mushrooms, if using, in a little light olive oil. Add a dash of tamari when they are nearly done.

Now, turn your grill on high and while it is heating up, stir the cream into the fennel, bring back to the boil and immediately remove from the heat. Stir in the mushrooms, if using. Sprinkle with the grated Parmesan and place under the hot grill until just bubbling. Serve at once.

Celeriac and porcini gratin

In less hurried times (about a lifetime ago), something like this would have taken a good hour and the rest. Layered up in the manner of gratin dauphinois and baked in a slow oven and relegated to the 'I would love to do it but it's too late and I don't have time so let's have fried eggs' slot. Aha, enter Nadine's favourite braising technique and there you have it – a melting, rich deliciousness in 30 minutes.

SERVES 4
20 g/½ oz dried sliced porcini mushrooms
2 tablespoons olive oil
1 onion, very finely sliced
1 head of celeriac, about 600 g/1 lb 5 oz, peeled and sliced very thin, either with a
    mandolin or with a very sharp knife, no more than 3 mm/⅒ inch thick
1 teaspoon bouillon powder
3 garlic cloves, very finely sliced
1 teaspoon lemon juice (optional)
sea salt and freshly ground black pepper
100 ml/3½ fl oz double cream
50 g/1½ oz Gruyère, grated
a few chives, finely snipped, or 1 tablespoon chopped parsley

First of all, put the porcini into a measuring jug with a little hot water to cover.

Heat the oil in a large frying pan or sauté pan. Add the onion and sweat for 2 minutes. Add the celeriac, 850 ml/1½ pints of water and the bouillon powder, garlic, lemon juice, if using, and a little pepper. Bring to the boil and bubble rapidly for 20 minutes, turning the celeriac regularly, until the liquid has evaporated and the celeriac is cooked.

After about 15 minutes, add the porcini and their soaking liquid to the celeriac, followed immediately by the cream. Continue to boil until the sauce is reduced to the consistency of double cream.

Preheat the grill to high.

Sprinkle the grated Gruyère over the creamy celeriac and porcini and place under the hot grill for about 2 minutes. Serve sprinkled with chives or parsley, with a green salad.

Aubergine and halloumi with coriander pesto

Aubergine's love of olive oil is paralleled by its need for salt and an astringent something to cut through that engorged oiliness. In this case, it's lime. The halloumi provides just the right salty, sharp edge. A Greek taverna, a hot summer's day, a warm breeze, all in an earthenware dish – well, actually, mine was Pyrex but still the imagination soars.

SERVES 4
2 large aubergines, cut into ½ cm/¼ inch thick slices
6–8 tablespoons olive oil
dash of Tabasco sauce
juice of 2 limes
400 g/14 oz halloumi, cut into ½ cm/¼ inch thick slices
2–3 tablespoons coriander pesto (page 15)
1 tomato, roughly chopped (optional)

Preheat the oven to its highest setting.

Heat a griddle pan or frying pan. Brush the aubergine slices with olive oil on both sides and griddle or fry until brown.

Sprinkle with Tabasco and most of the lime juice, reserving a little to add when you serve the dish. Layer the aubergines and halloumi in a large ovenproof dish, starting with aubergine, and spreading each layer with a little of the pesto. Add the chopped tomato on top, if using. (It is there primarily for colour so don't feel you have to, especially if you are also serving a tomato salad.) Cover with foil and bake in the oven for 10 minutes.

Remove the foil, sprinkle with the remaining lime juice and serve with warmed pitta, a green salad, and a tomato salad with some finely minced red onion.

index

R

S

acknowledgements

Thank you to Maggie Ramsay, my patient editor who let me bother her ten times a day but who didn't bother me at all, except to tidy me up. **Thank you** to my publisher Margaret Little, without whose vision and tenacity this book would never have happened. **Thank you** to David Rowley and Clive Hayball (the 'White Heat' team) for creating such an exquisitely designed book. **Thank you** to Annabel Ford, who tested one recipe after another with me and shopped and entertained Noah and made the whole thing such fun. **Thank you** to Bridget Sargeson for cooking the food for photography and having to deal with getting the recipes at such short notice. **Thank you** to Philip Webb for the stunning photographs and for running around with his camera to catch 'the' shot. **Thank you** to Sarah Cuttle, his assistant, for being so calm, patient and lovely all the way through. **Thank you** to Francesco Guidicini for the portrait. **Thank you** to Claudia for make-up. **Thank you** to Helen Trent for finding the props. **Thank you** to David at Fruit Arrow, who generously donated some of the vegetables for my home testing and to Poupart, who did the same. **Thank you** also to Cheese Cellar for supplying the wonderful cheeses, including the exquisite Golden Cross. **Thank you** to Sandra at The Delicatessen Shop in South End Green, Hampstead, who let me have a huge tray of fresh homemade pasta to play with. **Thank you** to Vernon at Cucina, also in South End Green, for getting me wild rocket and trevise and other things at short notice, and for his small but absolutely perfect stock of ingredients that I used to have to drive a mile for. **The end**.